A COLLECTION OF
Indo-global recipes
BOOK 3 DOLCE & TICKLERS
BY IRA GHOSH

BlueRose ONE
Stories Matter
NewDelhi • London

BLUEROSE PUBLISHERS
India | U.K.

Copyright © Ira Ghosh 2025

All rights reserved by author. No part of this publication may be reproduced, stored in a retrieval system or transmitted in any form or by any means, electronic, mechanical, photocopying, recording or otherwise, without the prior permission of the author. Although every precaution has been taken to verify the accuracy of the information contained herein, the publisher assumes no responsibility for any errors or omissions. No liability is assumed for damages that may result from the use of information contained within.

BlueRose Publishers takes no responsibility for any damages, losses, or liabilities that may arise from the use or misuse of the information, products, or services provided in this publication.

For permissions requests or inquiries regarding this publication, please contact:

BLUEROSE PUBLISHERS
www.BlueRoseONE.com
info@bluerosepublishers.com
+91 8882 898 898
+4407342408967

ISBN: 978-93-6452-060-7

Cover design: Yash Singhal
Typesetting: Namrata Saini

First Edition: February 2025

DEDICATION

I dedicate this book to my late husband Ashis Bindu Ghosh. When we married, I could barely cook! However, my culinary abilities grew and flourished through his constant encouragement and support (and unfailing good humour at some of my less successful creations). His career enabled us to live in different countries and experience and appreciate different cultures. Much later, after I had accumulated my varied collection of recipes from around the world, he encouraged me to share them through their publication. He was instrumental in getting the first version of my recipe collection into a publishable form. If it were not for his hard work, support, and encouragement, this book would not exist, and I would not have been able to share my recipe collection with you.

I also dedicate this book to my mother Ratnavali Baruah who was a very good cook and had some fantastic recipes. She however, never had any set formula. Before my marriage my mother always worried about my lack of culinary ability!

Additionally, I dedicate this book to my grandmother Pragna Sundari Devi who was the first person to author a series of systematic cookbooks in Bengali extending to several volumes. Her books were my constant reference abroad, from which I learnt my basics.

TABLE OF CONTENTS

Introduction 1
Weights, Measures, & Temperatures 3

SWEETS 7

Coconut Barfi (I) 9
Coconut Barfi (II) 10
Coconut Barfi (III) 11
Coconut Balls 12
New Zealand Coconut Ice 13
Jalebis 14
Semolina Barfi 15
Soya Barfi 16
Simple Sandesh (I) 17
Sandesh (II) 18
Quick Easy Sandesh (III) 19
Oven Sandesh 20
Rosogolla 21
Pressure-Cooked Powder Milk Rosogolla 22
Baked Rosogolla 23
Dil Bahar 24
Gulab Jamun (I) 25
Gulab Jamun (II) 27
Soya Powder Gulab Jamun 28
Lady Kenny 29
Channar Mishti Roll (Paneer/Cottage-Cheese Sweet Rolls) 30
Channar Mishti (Bengali Cottage Cheese Sweet) 31
Kheer Toast (Cream Toast) 32
Bread Hulwa 33
Egg Hulwa 34
Pumpkin Hulwa 35
Soya Bean Hulwa 36
Middle Eastern Semolina Hulwa (I) 37
Middle Eastern Hulwa (II) 38

Sweet Potato Hulwa 39
Left-Over Roti Hulwa 40
Rangaaloo (Sweet Potato) Pitha (I) 41
Sweet Potato Mishti (II) 43
Malpoa 44
Okinawa Sweet 45

DESSERTS 47

Rice Pudding 49
Delicious Rice Pudding Or Cake 50
Quick Semolina Dessert 51
Caramel Meringue With Peaches 52
Peach Or Pear Flambé 54
Pear Dessert 55
Stewed Pears 56
Pineapple Cream Dessert 57
Pineapple Rum Cream Dessert 58
Pineapple & Ice Cream 59
Banana Flambe 60
Baked Banana Splits 61
Piquant Melon Dessert 62
Chocolate Pudding 63
Malay Dessert 64
Tri-Coloured Dessert 65
Chocolate Rum Mousse 66
Chocolate Mousse 67
Pineapple Mousse 68
Lemon Cream 69
Lemon Sponge Cream 70
Pavlova 71
Pudim De Leite (Brazilian Milk Pudding) - Flan 72
Lemon Pancake Dessert 73
Somloi Galuska (A Rich Cake Dessert) 75
Mocha Dessert 77
Bhapa Doi Or Bengali Steamed Yogurt Dessert (I) 78
Bhapa Doi (III) 79

Bhapa Doi (III) 80
Yogurt Toffee Or Burfi Of Bhapa (IV) 81
Bengali Mishti Doi Or Sweet Yogurt (I) 82
Mishti Doi (II) 83
Mock Shrikhand 84
Ginger Marmalade Steam Pudding 85
Steamed Orange Pudding 86
Orange Sponge Pudding 87
Baked Guava Pudding 88
Steamed Guava Or Fruit Pudding 89
Guava Kheer 91
Simple Bread Pudding 92
Riki's Bread Pudding 93
Chocolate Bread Pudding 94
Plum Dumpling 95
Baked Or Pressure-Cooked Stuffed Apples 96
Mango Surprise 97
Mango Or Fruit Flan 98
Orange Flan 99
Orange Cups 101
Orange Cream 102
Cottage Cheese Dessert 104
Left-Over Frozen Dessert 105
Ambrosia 106
Bombé Alaska 107

ICE CREAMS 109

Basic Ice Cream 111
Simple Ice Cream 112
Vanilla Ice Cream 113
Chocolate Ice Cream 114
Lemon Ice Cream 115
Orange Or Any Other Fruit Ice Cream 116
Mango Ice Cream 117
Strawberry Ice Cream 118
Jack Fruit Ice Cream 119

Peppermint Ice Cream 120

Peanut Ice Cream 121

Patali (Solid Date Jaggery) Ice Cream 122

Rosomalai Ice Cream 123

Mock Ice Cream 124

Eggless Ice Cream 125

Mango Kulfi (Indian Eggless Mango Ice Cream) 126

CAKES 127

Floating Island (Cake) 129

Sembe (Maize) Cake (Tanzania) 130

Pound Cake 131

Marble Cake 132

Strawberry Delight 133

German Apple Cake 135

Chocolate Cake 136

Nut Cake 137

Stir Cake 138

Congo Cake 139

Feather-Weight Sponge 140

Sponge Gateau 141

Mocha Cake 142

Vienna Rolls 143

Tangy Sponge Cake 144

Sponge For Tortes 145

Plain Sponge Cake 147

Party Cup Cakes 149

Madeleines 150

Semlor (Swedish Cake) 151

Cream Cake (I) 152

Cream Cake (II) 153

Carrot Cake 154

Winter Sponge Cake 155

Easy Christmas Cake 156

Icebox Christmas Cake 157

Chocolate Icebox Cake 158

Spiced Wheat Cake 159
Delicious Whole Wheat Spice Cake 160
Chocolate Wheat Cake 161
Chocolate Sponge Cake 162
Chocolate Almond Cake 163
Patali (Date Jaggery) Cake 164
Cock-Eyed Eggless Chocolate Cake 165
Pastry Almond Cake 166
Besting Cake (German) 167
Plain Cake With Oil 168
Southeast Asian Casava Coconut Cake 169

COOKIES 171

Tasty Cookies 173
Csoroge (Hungarian) 174
Quick-Mix Chocolate Cookies 175
Chocolate Cookies 176
Chocolate Vanilla Cookies 177
Uncooked Chocolate Biscuits 178
Simple Home-Baked Cookies 179
Quick Simple Cookies 180
Biscuit Omelet 181
Light Vanilla Crescent Cookies 182
Marzipan Potatoes 183
Nankhatai (I) 184
Nankhatai (II) 185
Khourabia 186
Ginger Cookies 187
Ginger Thins -- Cookies 188
Maria's Cookies 189

Glossary 190
Alphabetical List of Recipes 195

INTRODUCTION

"*A Collection of Indo Global Recipes*", as the name suggests, is a collection of recipes that is influenced by my Indian background, as well as being the result of spending many years in different countries where my husband's job took me. While abroad, I actively participated in various international groups and made friends with people from many different countries.

I do not consider myself a great cook! However, I was always interested in collecting and devising new recipes and trying them out on friends and family. Their enthusiastic responses indicated that I must have been doing something right! Hoping that others might wish to enjoy the pleasure of cooking and experimenting with recipes from around the world with minimum effort, I decided to publish my collection. In addition to many of the Indian recipes I inherited or learned from my family, I have been building this collection since my husband's first international posting in 1967. I have also added to the collection recipes that I invented over this time. I have tried out all the recipes, and this book is the result of my explorations, collection, and experimentation. Many of the recipes have familiar names, but often prepared differently by various cooks. I tried to simplify each recipe, and in doing so built up a collection that is user-friendly. In a few recipes I could not forgo the temptation of using "ajinomoto" (MSG; monosodium glutamate) as this was a popular ingredient when I collected the recipes. In the intervening years, it was reputed to be harmful, but recently it has been classified by the U.S. Food and Drug Administration of being safe. However, if there is concern, ajinomoto may be replaced with a pinch of sugar to retain somewhat similar flavour.

I hope my work will be of use to many enthusiastic and curious cooks including the offspring of Indian diaspora living abroad, youthful techies wishing to serve party-fares, connoisseurs researching ethnic cooking, and adventurous cooks wanting to make good, interesting food with ease from diverse recipes. Some of the dishes remain time-consuming, but most can be made with a few quick and easy steps.

This book was a labour of love, and my family encouraged me through the years I took to complete this project. I published the first version of this collection, entitled "*A Collection of Recipes*" in 2012 in one large volume. My husband did the tremendous job of computerization and editing that version. However, before I could publish my book, I needed to first complete another important project. I had taken on the colossal task of editing the multi-volume cookbook in Bengali titled *"Amish O Niramish Ahar"* written by my grandmother Pragna Sundari Devi. My grandmother was the first writer of a systematic cookbook in Bengali. Her volumes were published starting from the year 1900 AD. My re-edited and re-arranged versions were published in 1995, after which I could concentrate on my recipe collection. In the years since I first published my collection, I have received feedback and added to it. It is now timely to re-edit and publish the current collection, but this time as a four-volume set to make it more accessible, user friendly, and with a slight change in title to reflect its roots in both Indian and international cuisines. My son, Dr. Richik Niloy Ghosh, was instrumental in helping me create this new four-volume version.

Many thanks are due to my relations and friends in India and abroad from whom I collected the original recipes, modified versions of which now appear in these pages. I am unable to thank them all individually. As my sources were from many nationalities using various units of measurements (metric, avoirdupois, and cups), I kept the units as were given in the originals. To assist the users, I have appended a conversion table covering the three systems. A glossary has also been added to help the reader to understand unfamiliar terms.

Bon Appétit

Ira Ghosh

29 February 2024

WEIGHTS, MEASURES, & TEMPERATURES

1. SOLID MEASURES

1 kg. (kilogram) = 1,000 gm. (gram) = 2.2 lb. (pound avoirdupois)

1 lb. = 16 oz. (ounce)

(a) Equivalent measures of some commodities

Avoirdupois measure	Commodity	Container equivalent
1 pound	Butter or other fat	2 cups
1 pound	Flour	4 cups
1 pound	Granulated or castor sugar	2 cups
1 pound	Icing or confectioner's sugar	3 cups
1 pound	Brown (moist) sugar	2 cups
1 pound	Golden syrup or treacle	1 cup
1 pound	Rice	2 cups
1 pound	Dried fruit	2 cups
1 pound	Chopped meat (finely packed)	2 cups
1 pound	Lentils or split peas	2 cups
1 pound	Coffee (beans)	2 cups
1 pound	Soft breadcrumbs	4 cups
½ ounce	Flour	1 level tablespoon
1 ounce	Flour	1 heaped tablespoon
1 ounce	Sugar	1 level tablespoon
¾ ounce	Butter	1 tablespoon smoothed off
1 ounce	Golden syrup or treacle	1 tablespoon
1 ounce	Jam or jelly	1 level tablespoon

(b) Dry volume/ weight measures

Container	Container	Volume	Weight
4 teaspoons (tsp.)	1 tablespoon	½ fluid ounce	14.3 grams
2 tablespoons (tblsp.)	⅛ cup	1 fluid ounce	28.6 grams
4 tablespoons	⅓ cup	2 fluid ounces	56.7 grams
5⅓ tablespoons	½ cup	2.6 fluid ounce	75.6 grams
8 tablespoons	½ cup	4 fluid ounces	113.4 grams
12 tablespoons	¾ cup	6 fluid ounces	170 grams (.375 pound)
32 tablespoons	2 cups	16 fluid ounces	453.6 grams (1 Pound)
64 tablespoons	4 cups	32 fluid ounces	907 grams (2 pounds)

2. LIQUID MEASURES

(a) Common usage

Measure	Measure	Measure	Volume
1 cup	8 fluid ounces	½ pint	237 millilitres
2 cups	16 fluid ounces	1 pint	474 millilitres.
4 cups	32 fluid ounces	1 quart	946 millilitres
1 pint	16 fluid ounces	½ quart	473 millilitres
2 pints	32 fluid ounces	1 quart	0.964 litres.
4 quarts	128 fluid ounces	1 gallon	3.784 litres
8 quarts	One peck		
4 pecks	One bushel		
dash	Less than ¼ teaspoon		

(b) Small quantities

1 teaspoon (US)	1/6 ounce	4.93 millilitres
1 tablespoon (US)	0.5 ounce	3 teaspoons
1 teaspoon (UK)	1.2 teaspoon (US)	6.16 millilitres
1 tablespoon (UK)	1.2 tablespoon (US)	18.48 millilitres
1 dessert spoon (UK)	2.4 teaspoons	12.32 millilitres
1 dash	~ ⅛ teaspoon	~ 0.6 millilitres

3. APPROXIMATE OVEN TEMPERATURES

Oven	Gas Regulo	Electricity	
		°F	°C
Cool	0 - ½	225 – 250	107 – 121
Very Slow	½ - 1	250 – 275	121 -135
Slow	1 - 2	275 – 300	135 – 149
Very Moderate	2 – 3	300 – 350	149 – 177
Moderate	4	375	190
Moderately Hot	5	400	204
Hot	6 – 7	435 – 450	218 – 233
Very Hot	8 - 9	475 - 500	245 - 260

Ovens might somewhat differ in their specifications.

SWEETS

COCONUT BARFI (I)

500 gm. desiccated coconut or fresh grated coconut

200 gm. jaggery or, molasses

Method

Cook coconut and jaggery in a heavy bottomed pan on low heat stirring all the time to prevent it from getting burnt. When the mixture forms into a ball and leaves the sides of the pan take off from the heat. Pour on a large flat well-greased plate. Spread evenly. Cut with a greased knife into diamond or any other shapes. Leave to cool. it will harden slightly. Store in a container in the refrigerator. Alternately, you can grease your palms and form into small balls while still warm. Cool on greased plate before storing.

COCONUT BARFI (II)

500 gm. fresh grated coconut or desiccated coconut

250 gm. sugar

2 gm. raisins well washed (optional)

1 tsp. cardamom pods

1 tsp. vanilla essence

Pink colour (optional)

Method

Mix all the above and cook, shape and store as "Coconut Barfi (I).

COCONUT BARFI (III)

Method

Proceed as coconut barfi (II). When half done, add 50 gm. or more '*khoa*' (thickened and solidified milk. This can be bought in most sweet meat shops). This should be broken up and well kneaded before adding to the coconut mixture. Alternately bring 2 litres milk to the boil. Reduce heat and keep stirring till milk is thick and reduced to $1/4$ of the quantity. Cool and mix with the coconut mixture. Keep cooking till barfi is done. Proceed as "Coconut Barfi (I) & (II).

COCONUT BALLS

250 gm. desiccated coconut

250 gm. castor or powdered sugar

250 gm boiled & mashed sweet potatoes

2-3 tblsp. cocoa

1 tblsp. grated lemon or orange rind

100 gm. raisins washed & soaked in 2-4 tblsp. rum

A little extra powdered sugar or desiccated coconut for covering the balls

Small paper cups

Method

Mix all the above and make into small balls the size of ping-pong balls or smaller.

Spread grease proof paper with either powdered sugar and coconut or half and half. Roll the coconut balls in this mixture and place in small paper cups and serve.

Variations: Instead of coconut you can use ground peanuts, cashew nuts or almonds. Instead of cocoa use a pink colouring. Proceed as above. Half coconut and half any kind of nuts may also be used.

NEW ZEALAND COCONUT ICE

1 kg. sugar

A pinch cream of tartar

1 tsp. butter

10 liquid oz. water

6 oz. desiccated coconut

1 drop pink food colouring

Method

Put sugar, water, and cream of tartar in a saucepan and boil for about 10 minutes. Remove from heat. Add coconut and butter and beat till very thick. If beating by hand use a wooden spoon. Grease a flat plate or tray. Spread half the mixture and smoothen out. Add pink colouring to the other half and spread on top of the white mixture quickly before sweet begins to set. Smoothen out top. Leave for 1 hour till set properly. Grease a knife or dip in cold water and cut into squares. Can be served after dinner or, with tea/coffee.

JALEBIS

5 cups flour sifted

½ cup chickpea flour (*besan*) sifted

Oil for frying

Water as required

A few drops of orange colouring

Method

Mix 4 cups sifted flour with enough water to make a creamy paste. Keep aside covered for about 3 days to let it ferment. If the weather is too hot, keep it for only 2 days. On the final day strain off the whey. To the paste add the rest of the flour and chickpea flour. Beat and mix well. if too dry add a little of the whey to get the right pouring consistency – not too thick and not too thin. Add the colouring. Pour mixture into a squeezy bottle with a hole at the mouth. Heat oil in a wok or deep pan to medium and drop swirls of *jalebis* in rings from the bottle. When bottle is empty fill with more of the mixture and continue frying in batches. Keep turning jalebis with a slotted spoon or they will brown unevenly. They should be a golden colour. Remove from oil when done and drain on paper towel. Dip in sugar syrup for a few min. till well penetrated. Should not be kept too long in the syrup or else they will become too soggy, soft and start to break. They should be crisp and sweet.

Sugar Syrup

4-5 cups sugar   2½-3 cups water

Boil sugar and water. Take scum off, if any, by adding a spoon of milk. Reduce heat and simmer for 10-15 minutes. Take off heat

----

SEMOLINA BARFI

1 cup fine semolina	1 litre thickened milk (1 litre boiled down to 1 cup)
1 cup cottage cheese (*paneer*)	1 tblsp. Heaped good ghee or, butter, or margarine
1 cup fine or castor sugar	1-2 silver foil sheets for garnish (optional)
2 tsp. raisins well washed and dried (optional)	

Method

Mix all the above ingredients together. (If desired, semolina may be slightly dry roasted on a griddle before mixing with the rest of the ingredients.) Place mixture in a heavy bottomed pan on low heat stirring with a wooden spoon occasionally till mixture leaves sides of pan and does not stick to the bottom. It should form a ball in the centre of the pan. Take off heat and spread on a greased plate or tray. Smoothen top and decorate with silver foil. Cut in diamond or square shapes. Can be stored in the refrigerator for about a week to 10 days.

SOYA BARFI

10 soya beans ground to a powder	1-1¼ lb. sugar powdered
¼ tsp. cardamom essence or, 12 tsp. cardamom powder	Milk as required
1-2 tblsp. raisins	¼ oz. butter

Method

Mix soya ground, sugar essence and enough milk to form a paste. Melt butter, add the soya mixture and raisins, and keep stirring on medium to low heat till mixture leaves the sides of the pan and forms a ball in the centre. Spread on a flat buttered dish about ¼ in thickness. Sprinkle powdered cardamom on top and decorate with silver paper. Leave to cool. Cut with knife into squares or diamond shapes. This sweet cooks very quickly. Be sure not to make mixture too stiff or it will be too hard and dry.

Variation: Cardamom can be substituted by any other flavouring e.g. cinnamon, nutmeg, mace, clove, mixed spice etc. etc. These can be added in powdered form. Slivered almonds or pistachios can also be added at the last minute of cooking and a little used for decorating.

SIMPLE SANDESH (I)

2 pt. milk plus 1-2 tsp. lime juice or, 1 cup cottage cheese

1 cup powdered milk

1 cup castor sugar

1 tblsp ghee or, butter oil.

Almonds for garnishing (optional)

Method

Bring milk to boil. Lower heat and gradually add the lime juice and keep stirring till the milk starts to curdle. Keep aside and cool. Strain well. (The water may be kept in the refrigerator for future use instead of lime juice. When the milk comes to boil add the sour water gradually till milk curdles.) Ready-made cottage cheese may also be used.

Mix all above ingredients including the curdled milk, except the ghee, well, till moist like *puri* dough. Heat ghee very slightly till melted in a heavy-bottomed pan on slow fire. Add above mixture and keep stirring until the right consistency. It should not be too dry. Turn out and spread on a greased plate – round, square, or oblong. Sprinkle with ground almonds if desired. Press down with another plate of similar shape. The mixture will harden very quickly. Cut with a knife dipped in cold water. Store *sandesh* in the refrigerator till required.

This *sandesh* does not take as long as some of the ones made by traditional methods. It is very convenient to whip up if guests are coming.

Variations:

1. **Strawberry Sandesh:** Add 2 tblsp. of strawberry crush or jam with the mixture – a deliciously flavoured *sandesh* with a delicate colour. The crush is always better. Can also use 2-4 tblsp. mashed fresh strawberries.

2. Similarly, different flavours may be added e.g. pineapple, chocolate, saffron etc

----

SANDESH (II)

2 lts. Milk	1 oz. *'pera'* (Indian sweet) or *'khoa'*

2 tblsp. sugar

Method

Make *paneer* from the milk. Mix *paneer*, *khoa* and sugar well. Cook on low flame in a heavy bottomed pan. Keep stirring preferably with a wooden spoon. When it is almost done raise the flame to dry off all the liquid. Do not let it burn. When mixture leaves the side of the pan take off the heat and add any flavouring and colouring. Let cool. Make any shape by hand or cookie cutter. May also spread on a plate and cut with knife into diamond shapes. Decorate with powdered almonds or pistachios or a combination of both. To make it a more party fare spread silver paper over the *Sandesh*.

QUICK EASY SANDESH (III)

1½ cup *paneer* (cottage cheese)

1 cup sugar

Colouring (optional)

1 cup milk powder

Strawberry essence or substitute (optional)

Method

Mix all the above well. Put mixture with the butter in a thick-bottomed pan over low heat. Keep stirring for about 5 or 10 minutes till mixture leaves the sides. Spread on a greased tray. When cool cut in squares and serve. Decorate top before cutting with bits of strawberry, powdered cardamom, or anything else that may catch your fancy.

OVEN SANDESH

2 litres milk

1 cup sugar

2 tblsp. ghee or, butter softened

1-2 tblsp. lemon juice or any other flavouring e.g. rose, cardamom, saffron etc.

1-2 sheets of silver paper for decoration

Method

Make cottage cheese (*paneer*) from the milk in the usual way. Mix well with the rest of the ingredients till smooth. Grease an oven-proof shallow dish. Place in a very slow oven. Take out of oven when set and let *sandesh* cool. Cut in squares or desired shapes. Decorate with silver paper. Add food coloring to the mixture if necessary, according to the flavouring of the *sandesh*. Store in the refrigerator if to be eaten later.

ROSOGOLLA

1 litre milk (preferably full-cream and fresh for best results)

3 cups sugar

½ tsp. tartaric acid or, as per instruction

4 cups water

Method

Bring milk to boiling point but do not let it boil. Take off heat and stir with a wooden spoon so that no top cream forms. Cool about 5 minutes. Now add tartaric acid or water from previous *paneer* kept in the refrigerator, stirring gradually till milk starts to curdle and *paneer* is formed. Do not add anymore tartaric acid. Strain and hang the paneer in a cloth for a couple of hours till all liquid has drained off. Knead well with fingertips and make into small balls- slightly larger than marbles. When cooked these balls will expand.

In a heavy-bottomed pan make sugar syrup with the sugar and water. Bring to boil and then lower heat. Add 1 tsp of milk to the syrup. If there is any scum it will come to the top which should be removed gently with a spoon. Now drop a few balls into the syrup keeping in mind that the *rosogollas* will expand and so leave space for this. Cover pan. From time-to-time sprinkle cold water on the *rosogollas* to make them spongy. The heat may have to be raised and lowered from time to time. During cooking do not let the syrup get too hot or the balls may break. The *rosogollas* are ready when the balls have little cracks or rather look like a sponge and feel light. Take the balls out and keep aside or in a bowl of cold water. Be careful they do not break. When all are ready put them back in the syrup and serve with the syrup. Can sprinkle a little rose water on the finished product. Store in the refrigerator till required.

PRESSURE-COOKED POWDER MILK ROSOGOLLA

2 cups cottage cheese made from full cream powdered milk

1-2 tsp. rose water

2 cups sugar

5 cups water

Method

Strain all the water out of the cottage cheese. Knead till smooth and soft. Form into round balls – a little larger than marbles. Keep aside. Make syrup with the sugar and water. Now, pressure-cook the *rosogollas* in the sugar syrup for 5 minutes. If necessary, pressure cook the *rosogollas* in batches. If the syrup is too much then keep boiling till reduced. Take the *rosogollas* out with a little syrup before reducing the syrup. Put the *rosogollas* back in the syrup when the desired quantity is reached. Sprinkle with the rose water.

BAKED ROSOGOLLA

10-12 Rosogollas

1 can condensed milk

1 cup milk or as needed

Method

Squeeze out the syrup from the rosogollas and then place the rosogollas in a dish – the rosogollas should not overlap. In a saucepan place the condensed milk; also rinse the condensed milk can with fresh milk and place in the saucepan. Cook the milk in low to medium heat until it thickens, stirring constantly so that it does not burn underneath. Pour the milk over the rosogollas and bake in a moderate oven until it sets and is slightly brown on top.

DIL BAHAR

8-10 large flat *rosogollas*

1 tblsp. almonds blanched and chopped fine

1-2 tblsp. small raisins (optional)

1 tsp. warm milk

1-2 tblsp. *khoa* powdered and sweetened

1-1½ cup thickened milk (*kheer*)

1 tblsp. pistachio blanched and chopped fine

A large pinch of saffron

1-2 sheets silver foil

Method

Make large flat *rosogollas* as the recipe given above or buy them from a shop. Can also use canned *rosogollas*. The *kheer* should be very thick and of spreadable consistency. It should not be dry like *khoa*. Cut *rosogollas* in half. Mix the kheer with all the nuts, raisins if used and the saffron diluted in 1 tsp. warm milk. Sandwich the *rosogollas* with this mixture. Lay the *Dil Bahars* on a flat dish and decorate with silver foil. Sprinkle with powdered khoa. This makes a great party dish for tea or as a dessert for lunch or dinner.

GULAB JAMUN (I)

1 cup flour sifted

4 cups full cream powdered milk

4 oz. ghee (clarified butter)

1 tsp. baking soda

½ cup yogurt

Oil for frying

Method

Sift flour and baking soda together. Add to the powdered milk. Mix with yogurt and ghee. Oil may be substituted instead of ghee. If mixture is too dry add a little fresh milk to get a good consistency to enable to roll into balls – do not make it too sticky. Take bits of dough between the two palms and press down. Then gently release pressure and begin to roll into small balls. Do not make the balls too big as they will increase in size once in the sugar syrup. The balls must be smooth and not develop any cracks which will mean, the mixture is dry. In this case it will either crumble or be too heavy.

Warm ghee or oil in a deep pan on medium temperature and deep fry the balls by constantly turning them. They should be evenly browned. Fry them in small batches and drain on paper towel. Now drop them into the sugar syrup which should be kept warm at all time, on very low heat. When the balls start to expand and become spongy gently put them in a deep serving bowl. Don't keep them in the syrup for too long or else they will crumble. While frying the jamuns if the oil gets too hot take pan off from direct heat and keep aside. Once the oil has cooled a little put it back on direct heat. The oil should not be too hot as the *gulab jamuns* will brown quickly but will be hard inside. If oil is again too cold, it will take too long to cook and may not be spongy when dropped into the sugar syrup. The frying of the *gulab jamuns* is the trickiest part. When all the *gulab jamuns* are done pour the sugar syrup over them into the bowl.

This can be served cold or warm with a little syrup. If the *gulab jamuns* are left over, store them covered in the refrigerator. They can be warmed on low heat with a little syrup as and when required.

(My Filipina friend liked them so much that she stored them in her deep freeze in several serving portions, thawing a few at a time and warming them up before serving!)

Sugar Syrup:

4 cups sugar   8 cups water

A pinch of saffron or, 1 tsp. rose water

Heat sugar and water in a deep pan till sugar melts and the whole comes to a boil. Throw in a little milk to let the scum, if any in the sugar, come up on top. Take scum off with a ladle. Now lower the heat to the lowest temperature. Add the saffron. If using rose water sprinkle just before pouring the syrup onto the *gulab jamuns* in the bowl.

GULAB JAMUN (II)

½ cup flour sifted

1 kg. *khoa* (boiled down dry milk) mashed

1 very small egg or,
1 egg yolk

2 tblsp. yogurt (more or less) for mixing

1 tblsp. candied or plain cardamom seeds

A pinch saffron or, 1-2 tblsp. rose water

Sugar Syrup:

2 cups sugar

4 cups water

Method

Make the syrup with sugar and water as the recipe for *gulab jamun* (1). Mix flour and khoya and bind with the egg. Add enough yogurt to make a smooth pliable dough. It should not be too dry or sticky. Make into small balls. Flatten balls slightly and press down in the centre with the thumb. Fill with 1-2 cardamom seeds, roll back into a ball and deep fry a golden brown. The oil should not be too hot or lukewarm. If too hot the jamuns will brown quickly but remain raw inside. If on the other hand the oil is not hot enough, the jamuns will disintegrate. The best method is to remove the oil from the heat once it gets too hot and fry the balls. As the oil starts cooling return the pan to the heat and keep frying. Once the *gulab jamuns* are done, drain on paper towel for a few minutes and then drop them into the syrup one by one very gently. Keep the syrup on very low heat till all the balls are done. Once in the syrup the balls will expand and become spongy. Remove and place them in another dish or they will break if left too long in the syrup. At the end, add saffron (if using) diluted in a little warm water and let blend for 2-3 mins. Take off heat and pour the warm syrup over the *gulab jamuns* in the dish. Alternately, sprinkle the rose water over the whole dish at this juncture. *Gulab jamuns* taste good, cold, or warm. Store in the refrigerator if not served immediately, till required. Take out the required number of *gulab jamuns* and heat on low in a little syrup, if preferred warm, as and when needed.

Note:

Khoa is available in most Indian sweet shops. Candied cardamom is usually available in groceries.

SOYA POWDER GULAB JAMUN

Method

This recipe is the same as the "Gulab Jamun (I)" recipe with a few changes. Substitute soya powder in place of milk powder. Use 2 tsp soda bicarbonate for every 2 cups soya powder. Omit the milk for mixing. Use more yoghurt if necessary. Soya Gulab Jamuns need to be warmed up every time before serving.

LADY KENNY

(The original version of this sweet must have been created for one Lady Canning, the Governor's wife, who appreciated it so much that it had to be named after her! However, this is just a distorted version of the original which is no less tasty considering it is only a home-made version.)

250 gm. cream cheese (*paneer*)	2 tblsp. semolina
½ tsp. bicarbonate of soda	1 tsp. good ghee melted
Raisins or, candied pink/white cardamom seeds	1-2 cups of oil for frying
¼ tsp. saffron diluted in 1 tblsp. warm water or 2 tsp. rose or *kewra* essence	½-1 cup sifted castor/icing sugar or finely powdered khoa

Method

Mix paneer, semolina, soda, and ghee and knead well. Form into 20 balls. Press the centre of each with the thumb and place either a raisin or a few cardamom seeds. Cover up and again roll between the palms and shape into either smooth balls or sausages. Heat oil to boiling point and then lower heat and keep at a medium constant temperature. Deep fry the *lady kennies* 4-5 at a time turning constantly so that they brown evenly on all sides. Drain on paper towels. Next drop them in sugar syrup and simmer on low heat for 15-20 minutes turning frequently. Take off heat, add saffron diluted in warm water or sprinkle rose/*kewra* essence, leave to cool, and rest for 2-3 hrs or till required. Serve the *lady kennies* with very little thickened syrup or take them out of the syrup and roll them in castor/icing sugar or powdered *khoa*. The latter is preferable.

Sugar Syrup:

1 cup sugar	3 cups water

Let sugar and water come to the boil. Lower heat and simmer for 15-20 minutes.

CHANNAR MISHTI ROLL (PANEER/COTTAGE-CHEESE SWEET ROLLS)

1 kg. cottage cheese	125 gm. fine semolina
1 tsp. baking powder or, soda (optional)	2 tsp. ghee
1-2 cups oil for frying	2 cups sugar
4 cups water	1 tblsp. rose water
1 tsp. saffron	½ tsp. cinnamon or, cardamom powder

Method

Mix cottage cheese, semolina, baking powder or soda, if using (makes the mishti lighter) and ghee. Knead for a couple of minutes till mixture is well blended and smooth. Shape into fingers about 1½" long or like cocktail sausages. Fry golden brown in oil which should not be too hot on medium low heat. Drain on paper towels.

In the meantime, make the syrup with the sugar and water. Let it come to boil. Remove all the scum from the sugar. Let syrup simmer on low heat. Drop the drained sausages gently into the syrup and keep on simmer till they swell and feel light to the touch. Remove carefully and place in a fairly wide deep dish. Pour the remaining syrup over them. Now sprinkle with any of the flavourings given above – rose water, saffron, cinnamon or cardamom. Two flavourings may also be used. When cool place in the refrigerator before serving.

CHANNAR MISHTI (BENGALI COTTAGE CHEESE SWEET)

3 cups cottage cheese	1 tsp. flour
1 tsp. fine semolina	1-2 cups oil for frying
3 cups sugar	6 cups water
1" stick cinnamon	

Method

Make the sugar syrup as in *rangaloo pitha* and keep aside. Knead the cottage cheese till smooth. Add the flour and semolina. Mix all well and shape into rounds or oblongs like the *rangaloo ptitha*. Deep fry till brown but not dark brown or black. Drain on paper towel Gently drop into the sugar syrup and keep overnight or for a whole day before serving, for the syrup to penetrate the *mishti*. Serve as in *rangaloo pitha*.

This sweet requires no filling. However, if desired coloured or plain white crystalised sugar balls can be placed in the middle. Any other filling can also be substituted. e.g. sweetened or unsweetened aniseed which adds to the flavour.

KHEER TOAST (CREAM TOAST)

1 cup (more or less) oil	20 slices of bread without crust cut in halves
2 cups sugar	4 cups water
A large pinch of saffron diluted	3 tblsp. sugar (optional)
1 tblsp. raisins	2 litres fresh milk boiled and reduced to ½ litre

Garnish:

A sprinkling of thinly slivered almonds or pistachios or both, rose petals, crystallized cherry halves, or silver foil.

Method

Heat oil and deep fry the bread slices an even golden brown 2 or 3 at a time. Drain on paper towel or brown paper. In the meantime, boil 2 cups sugar with the water. Reduce heat and keep the syrup on simmer. Add the saffron and let it dissolve. Now carefully lay the drained fried bread 2 or 3 at a time in the syrup and let it simmer for a few minutes. Do not let the bread get too soft or else it will break when removing from the syrup. Lift bread slices carefully from the syrup and arrange on a serving platter. Dissolve 3 tblsp sugar, if using, the washed and cleaned raisins with the reduced ½ litre of milk (*kheer*) during the last few minutes of boiling. Place 1 tsp of kheer on each toast and spread with a spatula or knife to cover the whole surface. Garnish with any of the above.

Variation

Instead of saffron or rose water, rose essence may be used in the syrup for flavouring.

BREAD HULWA

13-14 slices of bread broken	6-8 tblsp. good ghee or butter
1½ pt. fresh creamy milk	1 tsp. saffron
1 tsp. vanilla essence	½ tsp. cardamom powder
2 tblsp. heaped cleaned and washed raisins	5 tblsp. sugar
1-2 tblsp. extra butter or good ghee	1 tblsp. slivers almonds
1-2 sheets silver foil for garnishing	½-1 nutmeg powder for garnish

Method

Fry slices of bread brown in ghee or butter and keep aside. Heat milk with saffron, vanilla essence, cardamom powder, sugar, raisins, and almonds. Add fried bread to the milk mixture and crumble as much as possible. Keep cooking on moderate heat till the milk is absorbed. Add 1-2 tblsp butter or ghee to the mixture and keep frying on low heat till the mixture reaches a *hulwa* texture. Sprinkle with nutmeg (optional) and decorate with silver paper.

EGG HULWA

6-8 eggs	2 litres milk boiled down to approx. ½ litre
5 tblsp. butter or ghee	10 tblsp. sugar (approx.)
1-2 bay leaf	A few cardamom seeds
1 stick cinnamon	A handful of raisins
A handful of almonds blanched and sliced thinly	A pinch of saffron diluted in a little warm milk
1-2 sheets of silver foil	

Method

Separate and beat whites and yolks of eggs and then mix together in a heavy bottomed saucepan. Add the ½ liter milk, melted butter and all the rest of the ingredients except almonds and silver foil. Cook on low heat stirring continuously. Raise heat to medium towards the end of cooking only if necessary. Be sure the *hulwa* does not stick to the bottom of the pan. When *hulwa* becomes thick and set turn out onto a greased flat dish. Garnish with almonds and foil. Cut and serve.

PUMPKIN HULWA

1½ kg. red pumpkin peeled and cut small

250 gm. sugar

2" cinnamon stick or, 2 tsp. ground cinnamon

2 litres milk boiled down to ½ litre

2 tblsp. good ghee or butter

4 oz. raisins

4 oz. almonds blanched and cut in thin slivers

1 tsp. cardamom or cinnamon powder for garnish

2-3 sheets silver foil for garnish

Method

Pressure cook pumpkin. Drain all water thoroughly, mash or put in the food processor. Mix the sugar, cinnamon, milk, and pumpkin thoroughly. Return to medium to low heat. Cook stirring constantly till dry but mushy. Take off heat when ready and keep aside. In a heavy bottomed pan warm the ghee, add the pumpkin mixture along with the raisins and almonds keeping a few aside for decorating. Cook all stirring frequently, till dry and the mixture leaves the sides of the pan and resembles *hulwa*. Take off heat and spread on a greased flat dish. Sprinkle cinnamon or cardamom powder on top and/or a little almond shavings. Decorate with silver paper and leave to cool. Cut in small squares and serve hot or cold.

Cinnamon stick/powder may be substituted with 4-5 green cardamoms/2 tsp cardamom powder. Cinnamon gives a better flavour. A large pinch of mace and nutmeg powder also enhances the flavour.

Note:

The above may be used for a pie filling, in which case, flavour with one tsp. heaped mixed spice.

SOYA BEAN HULWA

Method

Soak the required amount of soya beans overnight. Next day wash several times to get rid of the skin. Purée beans in a blender or food processor. Now proceed making the *hulwa* the same as pumpkin or egg *hulwa*.

MIDDLE EASTERN SEMOLINA HULWA (I)

A handful of almonds sliced

¾ cup melted butter

1 cup sugar

Powdered cinnamon for garnish

1 cup semolina

2 cups milk

A few drops vanilla essence

Method

Fry the almonds and semolina in the butter stirring constantly till almonds turn brown. Be careful not to burn the almonds. Heat to boiling, the milk, sugar, and vanilla essence. Pour the latter over the semolina and stir. Cover with a cloth and then a lid. Cook over low heat till the liquid is absorbed. Stir frequently returning the cloth and lid after stirring. Place on a greased dish and sprinkle top with cinnamon.

MIDDLE EASTERN HULWA (II)

1 cup almonds shelled, blanched, and chopped

2 cups semolina

1 cup olive oil or ½ oil and ½ butter

2 cups sugar

3-4 cups water

1 stick cinnamon

1 cup milk

½-1 tsp. cinnamon powder

3-4 almonds shelled and slivered for garnishing

Method

Fry almonds and semolina in oil till light brown. Boil sugar, water, and cinnamon to make a light syrup. Add the syrup to the semolina and stir over low heat to blend. Add the milk and keep stirring till the mixture leaves the sides of the pan. Take off heat and cover pan with a cloth till cool. Sprinkle halva with cinnamon powder. Turn onto a buttered dish and level off the top. Garnish with slivered almonds. Serve cut into squares or triangles plain or with fresh cream.

SWEET POTATO HULWA

2 tblsp. flour

¼ tsp. cardamom powder

1 cup sugar

2-4 tblsp. butter/ghee/oil

A pinch saffron

2-3 almonds/pistachios chopped/slivered

1 tsp. baking soda

1 lb. sweet potatoes boiled mashed

2 cups water

2 tsp. or more raisins

1-2 tsp. rose water (optional)

1-2 sheets silver paper for garnish

Method

Sift the flour and baking soda together. Add the cardamom powder and mix. Add this to the sweet potato mash and mix all well till smooth and there are no lumps. Make syrup with the sugar and water and keep aside. In a deep-frying pan or wok fry the potato mixture in the butter till well browned. Add the sugar syrup, raisins and saffron, continue stirring till all the liquid is absorbed and the *hulwa* is set leaving the sides of the pan. Sprinkle rose water if using, stir and take off heat. Spread *hulwa* on a buttered flat dish about ½"-1" in height. Sprinkle chopped or slivered almonds on top and cover with silver paper. Serve cut in squares or as it is, at tea/coffee time or as a dessert with whipped cream.

LEFT-OVER ROTI HULWA

Soak 3-4 rotis in 1-1½ cups fresh warm milk or just enough to cover rotis for 2-3 minutes. When soaked, crumble the rotis. In the meantime, boil and thicken ½ liter or more milk down to half the quantity stirring frequently. Mix with the rotis along with flavourings- whole or powdered cinnamon/cardamom and about 3-4 tblsp castor or powdered sugar. Mix well. Heat 1-2 tblsp ghee or butter and cook the mixture as in Pumpkin *Hulwa*. Similarly add raisins, almonds, rosewater or/and saffron. Decorate with silver foil. Serve, without cutting in squares, with fresh cream as a dessert or as a tea-time snack minus the cream and cut in squares or slices.

RANGAALOO (SWEET POTATO) PITHA (I)

(This is a simple Bengali sweet dish, a favourite in many homes.)

   1 tsp. baking powder   2-4 tblsp. heaped flour

   1 kg. sweet potatoes boiled and mashed   1-2 cups oil for deep frying

Method

Sift the flour and baking powder and then mix with the prepared *rangaloo*. Knead well till smooth with no trace of any lumps. Take off bits from the dough and shape into rounds or oblongs the size of an index finger. Dust palms with flour from time to time while shaping to avoid sticking. Make a depression in the centre and place a little filling. Cover filling well so that no cracks appear. Deep fry 2-3 at a time depending on the size, in a deep-frying pan or wok till brown. Drain on paper towels   Drop the *pithas* in already prepared sugar syrup. Keep aside for 2-3 hours or overnight before serving so that they are well soaked. Sprinkle rose water or a little saffron diluted in water, if desired. It can be served with morning coffee, at afternoon tea or even as a dessert accompanied with "*kheer*" or "*rabri*".

Filling:

   1 cup good jaggery or molasses   2 cups or less desiccated coconut

Mix the above and cook over medium heat till well blended and sticky.

Sugar Syrup:

   2 cups sugar   4 cups water

   1" stick of cinnamon for flavouring

Cook all the above together on high heat till sugar melts stirring continuously. Reduce heat and let it simmer for about 10-15 minutes or threadlike consistency when dropped from a teaspoon. Take off heat and cool.

Variation:

1. ¼ cup "*khoa*" or 2 cups rich creamy milk boiled down to ¼ cup can be added to the filling to give it a richer consistency and added flavour.

2. **Mock Khoa** (see in "Miscellaneous chapter" of this book) is also a good substitute. Add raisins, nuts, and pine sugar to it.

3. Cottage or cream cheese, raisins, palm *jaggery* or fine sugar, mixed together can also be used as a filling.

SWEET POTATO MISHTI (II)

2 lbs. sweet potato boiled and mashed

2-4 tblsp. of flour

1 tsp. baking powder

1 lb. cottage cheese

½ lb. palm *jaggery*

1-2 tblsp. oil

Method

Mix all the above ingredients, except the oil, together and knead well till dough is smooth. Form into balls size of a golf ball (more or less), flatten or make a slight depression in the centre with the thumb. Brush tops with oil. Place on a greased baking tray and bake in a medium hot oven for 15–20 minutes or till done. Test by inserting a skewer or fork in the centre which should be dry when taken out. Turn the baking tray around from time to time to get an even golden-brown colour. Roll in castor sugar while still hot and serve.

Variations

1. Mix ¾-1 cup butter/margarine or 4-6 tblsp, oil with the dough. In this case no need to brush the tops of balls with oil anymore.
2. Add a handful of raisins to the dough.
3. Serve the balls sprinkled with honey or any syrup – maple or liquid palm *jaggery* (*nolen gur*). In this case no castor sugar is necessary.

MALPOA

1 cup flour

½ cup cottage cheese

A pinch of saffron

1 cup sugar

Oil for frying

¼ tsp. baking soda

½ cup condensed milk

1 tsp. aniseed

2 cups water

Method

Sift flour and baking soda together. Add the cottage cheese and condensed milk and saffron. Mix all well or put through a food processor till smooth. Now add the aniseed and stir to mix. Make the sugar syrup with the sugar and water to two thread consistency. Keep aside in a warm place. Warm enough oil to cover a heavy bottomed fry pan. Place batter in the fry pan with a rounded soup spoon spreading a little from the centre in a circular motion. The *malpoas* should not be too thick or too thin – about 4" in diameter – need not be a perfect round and could have jagged ends. The *malpoas* should be fried a golden brown. When bubbles appear on one side turn them over till bubbles appear on the reverse side. Fry the *malpoas* in small batches. Take off heat and drain on paper towels for a few minutes. Drop *malpoas* in the warm sugar syrup and leave till soft. Carefully lift them out of the syrup and serve. The excess syrup can be refrigerated till required for some other use. The above batter should make 12 *malpoas*.

OKINAWA SWEET

2 cups sweet potato steamed and mashed   1 cup brown sugar

1½ cups potato flour/corn starch/corn flour   Oil for deep frying

Method

Mix all the above ingredients and form into tiny balls the size of marbles or a little bigger. Flatten the balls slightly by pressing them in between the palms. Deep fry in oil. Drain on paper towels and serve warm. The balls can be rolled in icing or castor sugar if so desired.

DESSERTS

RICE PUDDING

2 cups rice

2-3 tblsp. sugar or, to taste

2-3 eggs (if no 'hang-ups' about eggs use 4-5) separated

1 litre milk

1 tsp. vanilla essence

Breadcrumbs for sprinkling

Method

Cook rice in milk. When ready take off heat and cool. Add the sugar and the vanilla essence and mix till dissolved. Now add the egg yolks. Mix well. Grease a round mould or cake tin. Spread bottom of dish with breadcrumbs. Pour the rice mixture into the mould. Beat the egg whites stiff and spread evenly on top. Bake in a moderate oven till golden brown. Serve with cream.

Variations

1. Omit the vanilla. Replace with 2 tblsp cocoa or, 3-4 tblsp desiccated coconut.

2. Divide the mixture into 2 parts. Flavour half with vanilla and the other half with 1 tblsp. cocoa or, a combination of cocoa and coconut. When ready cut in slices

3. Instead of spreading egg whites on top it can be folded into the mixture at the last minute. If flavouring with half vanilla and half cocoa, add the whites before adding the cocoa.

4. For extra flavour add 2 tblsp. brandy or rum.

DELICIOUS RICE PUDDING OR CAKE

(This is an interesting version of the ever-popular rice pudding which could be served as a dessert or as a cake with tea or coffee.)

1 litre milk	10 oz. vanillin sugar or, a mixture of plain sugar with 1-2 tsp. of vanilla essence
1 or 2 cups of grated coconut	2 cups rice
1 to 2 tblsp. raisin	3-4 egg yolks

Method

Cook milk, and half the sugar and coconut together with the rice in a saucepan till rice is done and all the milk has been absorbed. Cool. Now mix the yolks, raisins, and rest of the vanillin sugar. Grease a baking dish. Sprinkle with breadcrumbs or semolina. Pour rice mixture into this dish. Bake in medium hot oven for about $\frac{1}{2}$ hour take out, spread meringue on top and return to medium oven till done. Meringue should be evenly golden brown. Serve hot or cold with or without fresh cream.

<u>Meringue:</u>

3-4 egg whites	3-4 tblsp* castor sugar
2 tblsp. any plain jam	* Depending on the number of eggs used

Beat egg whites and sugar till stiff. Add jam and beat a little more. Quickly spread on cake.

Variations

Instead of using all grated coconut use only 1 cup while cooking with the milk and rice. Continue as above. Cool. Divide the rice mixture into 2 sections. Add 1-2 tsp vanilla and pink colouring to one section and 4 oz. sweet chocolate to the second section. Sandwich together in the baking dish in the following manner – chocolate first and then vanilla. If desired the coconut may be completely omitted. Divide rice after cooking with only milk into 3 sections. Add only 1/3 of the coconut to one section of the mixture and mix well. Cook for a few seconds. Cool. Place at the bottom of the baking dish. Add chocolate to the second part of the rice and milk mixture which should go in the middle. Add vanilla to the last section and place on top. Now continue as above.

QUICK SEMOLINA DESSERT

3 eggs

1 litre milk

1 tsp. vanilla essence

8 tblsp. sugar

6 tblsp. heaped semolina

Method

Beat egg yolks with half the amount of sugar. Bring milk to the boil. Add semolina and cook together on low heat for about 2-3 minutes. Take off heat and add to the yolk mixture very slowly beating all the time to get a smooth consistency. The mixture should not curdle or form lumps. Beat egg whites and the rest of the sugar till stiff. Fold in gradually to the semolina mixture with the vanilla. Serve hot or cold. It tastes better served cold. Alternately, place the mixture in an ovenproof dessert dish. Place this in a pan of water and bake in a pre-heated medium low oven for about 5 minutes.

Note

The water in the pan should come only halfway up the dessert dish or else the water may boil into the dessert.

CARAMEL MERINGUE WITH PEACHES

Caramel Meringue:

6 oz. castor or, powdered sugar	4 egg whites beaten stiff
3 oz. caramelized sugar powdered	

Peach Dessert:

4 ripe peaches halved	2-3 tblsp. castor/powdered sugar
1 tblsp. Marsala wine/rum/cognac/liqueur	1" piece cinnamon
1 tsp. corn flour	$1/4$-$1/2$ cup cottage/cream cheese mashed
1 tsp. vanilla essence	

Method

Add the castor sugar gradually to the egg whites. Next add the caramel sugar gradually. Line a large baking sheet preferably non-stick with foil or grease proof paper. Drop meringues on the tray by a teaspoon or dessert spoon depending on the size required. While dropping the meringues swirl the spoon to form peaks on top. Place in a low oven for approx. 5 minutes. (more or less). Switch off oven but leave meringues inside for another few mins till dry. Keep aside till required,

Place peach halves on a flat oven proof dish or baking tray. Sprinkle with 1 tblsp sugar and the wine. Place the cinnamon in between. Place in a low oven for 30–40 minutes till the peaches are soft but not squashy. Place the peaches after draining off all the syrup on a serving dish or individual dessert bowls. Put the syrup with the scrapings from the tray in a saucepan and place over gentle heat. Add the corn flour mixed in a little syrup or water and keep stirring continuously till it begins to thicken. No lumps should form. Pour syrup over the peaches. Combine the cheese, remaining sugar, and essence. Whip till smooth. Divide and place on the peach halves as a topping. Serve with the caramel meringues.

N.B. If using canned peaches use the syrup from the can to make the sauce adding the stick of cinnamon. The peaches can be placed directly on the serving dish or bowls and do not require to be cooked in the oven. Sprinkle with the *marsala* and continue as above. The sauce made from the syrup will not require any additional sugar. Also lessen the sugar in the topping.

PEACH OR PEAR FLAMBÉ

1 large can peach or pear	8-10 toasted or sliced almonds
¼ cup brandy	

Sauce:

½ cup juice from any of the above fruit can	1 tsp arrowroot, corn starch or corn flour
½ cup curaçao or any other liqueur.	A drop of edible green colouring (optional) depending on the liqueur used.

Method

Lay the contents of the can (keep ½ cup juice aside for the sauce) in a shallow oven-proof dish neatly. Sprinkle the almonds evenly on top. Mix all the sauce ingredients and heat till thick. Cover fruit with this sauce. Heat brandy and quickly pour over all and flambé. Serve immediately before the flambé dies out, with cream if desired.

Variation

1 large can of mango or orange slices may be substituted instead of peach or pear.

PEAR DESSERT

1 large can of pears (12-16 oz.)   2 eggs

8 oz. sugar   8 oz. butter or, margarine

6 oz. almonds blanched and ground

Method

Drain pears of all liquid and pack close together in a buttered oven-proof dish. Beat egg and sugar together well till smooth. Add butter and continue to beat till well incorporated with the egg/sugar mixture. now add the almonds and mix well. Should resemble a smooth paste. Cover pears with this mixture evenly and bake in a moderate oven for 25-30 minutes. Serve with fresh cream.

STEWED PEARS

8 oz. fresh pears skinned, cored, and halved/quartered

½ tsp. cinnamon powders

1 tblsp. brandy or, ½ tsp. brandy essence

2 tblsp. brown sugar

¼ tsp. each clove, mace, and nutmeg powders

Method

Mix the pears with all the above ingredients. Steam pears in a steamer or place in a container with a tight-fitting lid and pressure cook for 15-20 minutes. Serve with meringues, macaroons, fresh cream, or custard.

PINEAPPLE CREAM DESSERT

(Make this dessert 24 hrs. before serving. It is fairly light and a good end to a moderately heavy dinner.)

8 tblsp. (heaped) icing sugar	8 egg yolks
2 tblsp. (heaped) gelatine powder	½ cup cold water
1 cup (more or less) pineapple juice	3 slices canned pineapple cubed
2 oz. cream (whipped)	

Method

Beat sugar and yolks for 5-7 minutes or till light and frothy. Dissolve the gelatine in the water and leave for about 10 minutes to rest. Bring the pineapple juice to the boil. Immediately add the dissolved gelatine and keep on stirring till smooth. This should not become lumpy. Take off heat and let it cool. Pour into the sugar and yolk mixture. Stir to mix well making sure the mixture does not curdle. For this reason, the syrup should be absolutely cold before adding it to the sugar and yolk mixture. Stir in the pineapple cubes and then the whipped cream. Rinse a dessert bowl in cold water. Do not wipe the inside. Line the dish with cling-wrap leaving a little of the paper hanging over the edge all around the bowl – about 5 cm. Pour the dessert into the bowl and cover top with more cling-rap. Refrigerate for a day. From time to time stir dessert while in the refrigerator to prevent the pineapple cubes from sinking to the bottom. Take out of the refrigerator ½ hour. before serving. Un-mould and cut in slices. Serve with more pineapple slices and/or fruit salad.

PINEAPPLE RUM CREAM DESSERT

1 large ripe pineapple

2-4 tblsp. rum

Castor sugar only if required according to taste

1 cup thick cream

½-1 tsp. ginger powder

Method

Cut a thin slice from the bottom of the pineapple without cutting right through so that it can sit on a tray or flat dish without toppling. Now cut the top and keep it in reserve. Scoop out all the pineapple from the centre and cut in small cubes. Do not discard the juice. Gently mix the cream, rum, ginger, and sugar if using, and a little bit of the juice, if necessary, with the pineapple. Do not make the mixture too soggy. Cool in the refrigerator till required. Before serving fill the pineapple shell with the mixture and cover with the top. Make sure the pineapple top has some of the leaves.

Variation

¼ cup crystallized or maraschino cherries cut in half may be added to the pineapple.

PINEAPPLE & ICE CREAM

1 medium ripe pineapple

¼ tsp. ground ginger if using vanilla ice cream

1 brick vanilla or ginger ice-cream (bought or homemade)

2 tblsp. lemonade concentrate

Method

Prepare the pineapple shell as the "Pineapple rum cream dessert". Scoop out the pineapple gently keeping them as whole as possible. Cut the pineapple in thin slices. Gently toss with the ginger and lemonade. Fill the shell alternately with a little ice-cream followed by pineapple slices. Cover with ice-cream before replacing the shell cover. Freeze the whole till required. Place on a flat dish surrounded by the extra pineapple slices tossed in ginger and lemonade. Serve extra ice-cream separately. A simple, easy to make, cool, and delicious dessert to end a dinner on a hot summer evening.

BANANA FLAMBE

(This popular recipe of a light but elegant dessert after a heavy meal, has passed through many hands before reaching my 'repertoire' with several changes and alterations taking place on the way!)

6-8 large bananas (depending on the number of guests)	2-4 tblsp. lemon juice
1-2 tsp. lemon rind (approx.)	¼ tsp. mixed spice (optional)
¼ tsp. heaped cinnamon powder	¼ tsp. heaped nutmeg powder
¼ tsp. heaped clove powder	1 demitasse cup brandy/rum
2-4 tblsp. butter	½-¾ cup brown sugar

Method

Peel and remove thread from banana. Slice the bananas in half down the middle lengthwise and then cut each slice in half. Arrange the slices cut side down in a well-buttered shallow oven-proof dish. Sprinkle enough lemon juice mixed with a little of the rind over the banana slices to prevent discolouring and for a subtle lemony flavour. Combine the sugar with all the spice powders and sprinkle over the bananas evenly. Dot with blobs of butter and, place dish under the broiler/grill for approximately 5-8 minutes. Place the brandy/rum in a wide saucepan with a long handle. Put a little more of the lemon rind into it and stir to mix. Do not put too much rind. Warm the alcohol, remove from heat, and immediately pour over the bananas. This can be done on the side in front of the guests. Alternately bring the dessert out to the guests before the flame dies out. Serve immediately either by itself or with cream/ice-cream

Variations

The bananas can be substituted with any of the following fruits cut in segments, slices, or cubes according to the above directions – oranges, stewed apples or pears, pineapples etc. A cocktail of these fruits can also be used with a few cherries thrown in.

BAKED BANANA SPLITS

6-8 large bananas (depending on the number of guests)

24-28 large marshmallows

¾ cup or more pineapple (fresh/canned)

Method

Peel and remove threads from bananas. Split bananas lengthwise and then cut each slice in half. Butter a shallow oven-proof dish and place the banana slices cut side down, side by side in it. They should not over-lap. Chop, crush, and drain the pineapples and then cover the bananas with them completely. Next cover the pineapples with the marshmallows. Bake in a pre-heated moderate oven for about 10-15 minutes or till the marshmallows are melted. Serve hot as a dessert with cream or ice-cream.

PIQUANT MELON DESSERT

1-2 ripe melons (any kind)

1 tblsp. lemon juice

A dash of rum/brandy/sherry/any kind of liqueur

2 tblsp. sugar

½-1 tsp. ginger powder

Method

Peel melon and then cut in cubes or rounds with a marble shaped scoop. Mix with all the above ingredients and refrigerate for several hours. Serve garnished with cherries or cream. This is a good summer dessert.

CHOCOLATE PUDDING

4 oz. chocolate (preferably strong, dark, and sweet

3-4 tblsp. water

1 cup double cream

1 tblsp brandy (preferably cognac)

1 tblsp. vanilla essence

Method

Place chocolate with water in a saucepan and cook, constantly stirring with a wooden spoon, till melted. Let it cool. Whip cream and fold into the chocolate mixture with the vanilla and brandy. Pour into a dessert bowl or individual dessert dishes and chill. Just before serving garnish with a cream whirl and a sprinkling of chocolate nibs (grated chocolate).

This is a perfect ending to a gourmet dinner.

Variations

1. This pudding can be used as a filling for a pie or to sandwich a plain sponge or a chocolate sponge cake. Either sprinkle with icing sugar or ice with an icing of your choice. The pie may be garnished with swirls of cream and sprinkling of chocolate nibs.

2. For a mocha flavour, add 1-2 tsp. instant coffee with the vanilla and brandy.

MALAY DESSERT

5 eggs separated

10 oz. thick coconut milk

A large pinch of grated nutmeg

A very small pinch of salt

500 gm. *jaggery*

¼ tsp. cardamom powder

A large pinch of cinnamon powder

Method

Beat both yolks and whites separately and then beat together well. Mix finely scraped '*jaggery*', coconut milk, all the spices and salt. Be sure that all the ingredients are well blended. Pour into a greased heat-resistant mould. Cover with grease proof paper and steam either in a pressure cooker or steamer for approximately 1¼ hours or till firm. If steaming in a pressure cooker it should take about ½ hr. This dessert maybe served either in the mould or un-moulded on a platter with or without cream. To unmould, loosen the sides with a sharp knife and when cool invert onto the serving platter.

TRI-COLOURED DESSERT

4 large farm fresh eggs separated	9½ oz. castor sugar
3 level tsp. gelatine	Water as required
3 tblsp. rum, brandy, or sherry	2 tsp. instant coffee
2 tblsp crème de menthe (green)	1 cup double cream
2 tblsp. castor sugar	1 tsp. vanilla essence
2-3 tblsp. chocolate nibs	

Method

Beat egg yolks with the 9½ oz. of sugar till fluffy, light and lemon coloured. Dissolve gelatine by first putting 1 tsp cold water in a small bowl. Add gelatine to it with just enough water to cover it. Beat egg whites stiff like meringue. Add this to the yolk mixture folding in with a wooden spoon alternately with the rum, brandy, or sherry, one tablespoon at a time. Divide the mixture into three. Add the coffee to one and the crème de menthe to the other. Leave the third plain. Fill a dessert bowl with cold water and then throw it out. Do not dry inside of bowl. Fill the bottom of the bowl with the plain mixture and refrigerate for approx. 5 minutes, turning the temperature to maximum cold. Next top it with the crème-de-menthe mixture and again keep it in the refrigerator as the plain mixture. This is necessary so that the colours of the different mixtures do not run into each other. Each addition of mixture may be kept in the cool for more than 5 minutes if necessary. The different mixtures while waiting to be added to the main whole may be set aside in the bottom shelf of the refrigerator to facilitate the actual setting in the end. Last of all add the coffee mixture and keep dessert in the refrigerator overnight.

Next day invert dessert on a flat serving dish. Cover with beaten cream, sugar, and vanilla. Sprinkle with chocolate nibs. Keep in the refrigerator till required.

Variations

A mixture of half sherry and half orange curaçao may be added to the basic mixture instead of only rum, brandy, or sherry.

CHOCOLATE RUM MOUSSE

6 oz. sweet chocolate

1 tsp. vanilla

1 tbsp. hot water

2 tblsp. rum

5 large eggs separated

1 tsp. instant coffee

½ pt. double cream

Method

Melt chocolate in a double boiler which should have hot but not boiling water. Remove from heat and cool but not too cold. Beat egg yolks slightly and then beat it into the chocolate. Add vanilla and the coffee diluted in the hot water. Beat cream until thick. Add rum and fold into the chocolate. Beat egg whites stiff and gradually fold into the mousse. Rinse a dessert bowl in cold water. Do not dry the inside. Pour mousse in the bowl and cool in a refrigerator. Before serving decorate with grated chocolate.

CHOCOLATE MOUSSE

2½ cup butter unsalted

6 egg yolks

6 egg whites

Fresh strawberries for garnish (optional)

1 cup heavy whipped cream

2 cups super fine granulated sugar

4 oz. plain sweet chocolate melted over hot water and mixed with an additional 1 tblsp. butter

¼ cup cognac

1½ cups walnuts finely chopped

Method

In a large bowl beat butter and sugar together with an electric hand blender on high speed for 20 minutes. Alternately beat in the food processor. Add egg yolks one at a time. Gradually beat in melted hot chocolate with the additional butter. Beat for another 3 minutes longer. Add the cognac and beat an additional 3 minutes. Mix in the nuts. Beat the egg whites stiff in another bowl. Fold into the main mixture and blend well. Set in a ring mould. Refrigerate for 3 hrs. Gently turn out onto a serving dish. Decorate top, sides and hollow with cream and strawberries

----

PINEAPPLE MOUSSE

1 can evaporated milk

1½ cup water

1 tblsp. custard powder

2 tsp. heaped gelatine powder

½ can condensed milk

1 medium fresh pineapple stewed and chopped fine

Method

Put unopened can of evaporated milk in a pan of boiling water and continue boiling for 15-20 minutes. Take off heat, cool and keep in the freezer compartment. This should be done 2-3 days ahead of the day required. Open can and beat the milk. Dissolve the gelatine in ½ cup water. Add to milk and beat some more till well mixed and smooth. Dilute the condensed milk with the rest of the water over med. heat. Take off heat when well blended. Add the custard powder and whisk well. Add the cooked pineapple minus the water. Beat well. Add this mixture to the evaporated milk mixture and beat all well again till well blended. Mould and refrigerate till set. Decorate with pineapple bits and chopped nuts. Colour the nuts if desired.

Variations

1. Instead of using fresh pineapple substitute canned pineapple minus the syrup. Any other fresh or canned fruit may also be used.

2. Instead of fruit 1-2 tblsp cocoa or 1-2 tblsp strong coffee may be used. Decorate with cherries and almonds.

LEMON CREAM

4 eggs	4 oz. sugar
4 tblsp. fresh lemon juice	¼-½ tsp. lemon rind grated
1 tblsp. brandy	4 sheets gelatine or, 4 tsp. heaped gelatine powder
3-4 tblsp. hot water	Thin lemon slices and cherries for garnish
Cold water as required	

Method

Separate eggs. Beat the yolks with the sugar till latter is dissolved and the mixture is of a creamy consistency. Add lemon juice, rind and brandy and stir to mix. Soak gelatine sheets in cold water just enough to cover and soak well for about 10 minutes. Take sheets out and squeeze all the water out. Throw away the cold water and add about 3-4 tblsp. hot water to the gelatine. Leave till gelatine is completely dissolved. Alternately soak gelatine powder in 3-4 tblsp. of hot water till dissolved. When cold add to the egg mixture. Do not let gelatine become rubbery. Stir a couple of times, if necessary, while soaking. Stir or beat mixture lightly into the egg mixture to blend. Put in the refrigerator for about 10 minutes or till set. Take out of the refrigerator and fold in the egg whites stiffly beaten. Put in a mould and refrigerate till set. Unmould and cover with well-beaten fresh cream. Decorate with thin lemon slices and cherries. Keep in the refrigerator till required.

LEMON SPONGE CREAM

2 lb. sponge/angel cake crumbled

2-4 tblsp. rum

½ litre double cream

2 tblsp. gelatine

¾-1 cup fresh lemon juice

1-2 tblsp. lemon rind grated fine

2-4 tblsp. castor sugar

4 tblsp. cold water

Method

Soak the crumbled cake with the lemon juice and rum. Use more juice or rum if necessary, taking care not to overdo it! Mix well with a wooden spoon till mushy. Stir in the lemon rind gently to the mixture. Beat the fresh cream and castor sugar well before adding to the cake mixture. Keep aside. In a small bowl soak gelatine in the cold water. Place it in a larger bowl of hot water and keep stirring till gelatine is dissolved and is of a clear transparent consistency. Add to the cake mixture and mix well till blended. Butter a large dessert bowl and pour cake mixture into it. Place in the refrigerator to set. Just before serving turn pudding on to a flat dish. Garnish sprinkled with finely grated lemon rind.

Variations

1. **Orange Sponge Pudding:** Same as above only substitute fresh orange juice or orange concentrate in place of lemon juice. If oranges are sweet omit or reduce the amount of castor sugar from the cream. Garnish with grated orange rind or/and chopped or whole oranges.

2. **Fruit Sponge Pudding:** Same as above but substitute 1 small can of any fruit with a strong flavour (e.g. peaches, apricots etc). Save a few pieces of fruit for the garnish.

PAVLOVA

6 large egg whites

1½ cup castor sugar

3 tsp. vinegar

Pinch of salt

3 tsp. corn flour

7 drops pink colouring or any essence

Method

Beat the egg whites with salt till stiff. Gradually add sugar and continue beating all the while. Fold in the corn flour and vinegar. Add the colouring or essence. Line a cookie or flan sheet with greaseproof paper. Pour mixture onto this like a flan. With a wooden spoon put some of the mixture as blobs on top. Smoothen out the inside of the flan with a palette knife. Bake for 15 minutes in a fairly low oven - 250^0 F. Then lower temperature to 200^0 F and continue baking for about 1¼ hours. Cool in oven overnight. Can be stored in an airtight container. Before serving fill with cream and strawberries or jelly and grapes or banana and sherry mixture.

PUDIM DE LEITE (BRAZILIAN MILK PUDDING) - FLAN

(This is a version of the ever popular 'caramel custard' – delicious!)

4 eggs	1 regular can condensed milk
8 oz. (liquid) fresh milk (more milk could be added for a less sweet dessert)	5 tblsp. sugar
2 tblsp. water	

Method

Break eggs one at a time in a bowl. Mix gently but do not beat at any cost. Mix well the condensed milk and the fresh milk together. Pour this into the eggs gradually, stirring continuously till all well blended and smooth. Just mix – do not beat at any stage. Keep aside. Heat sugar in a saucepan till it dissolves and turns a golden brown. Quickly add the water and pour into an oven-proof dessert bowl. Turn the bowl around so that the caramelized sugar coats the bottom and all the sides of the bowl. If the sugar hardens during the process, quickly return the pan to the heat. As soon as the sugar starts melting again, continue with the above process without wasting time. This is the most difficult part of the dessert Now pour the egg/milk mixture over the caramelized sugar in the bowl. Put the bowl in a pan of water which comes a little less than halfway up. Bake in a mod oven for about 1 hr or till set. Test by inserting a toothpick in the centre of the pudding which should come out clean. If the pudding shakes too much, then it is not ready. When the dessert is done and is still hot, cover with a serving plate, hold tight and turn upside down. It will now rest on a serving dish. Fill all the crevices with spoons full of the juice from the caramel. If desired garnish with a sprinkle of minced cherries and almonds which should be dry roasted first.

Variation

For an easy version of 'Crème Brûlée, sprinkle top of dessert with the sugar and brown evenly under a broiler or grill. No need to caramelize at the early stage.

LEMON PANCAKE DESSERT

½ cup flour sifted

1 tblsp. fine sugar

1 egg well beaten

½ pt. milk or, as required

2-4 tblsp. corn flour sifted (optional)

A pinch of salt

2 tsp. melted butter

Extra melted butter or, oil for making the pancakes

Method

Mix flour, corn flour, sugar, and salt together. Add the melted butter and stir. Next add the beaten egg one at a time and beat well. Add enough milk to make the batter reach a pouring consistency. This whole operation becomes easier done in a food processor. Brush a small non-stick pan or skillet with oil. Pour a little batter onto the skillet and spread thinly with the back of a spoon. When bubbles appear on the surface turn it over for a few seconds. Peel off and store in between a sandwich cover till all done.

Lemon Curd:

4 oz. butter or margarine

2 large eggs

4-6 oz. fresh lemon juice strained

8 oz. sugar

2 tsp. lemon rind finely grated

Melt butter and sugar in a double boiler or in a saucepan over boiling water. Beat in the eggs well. Add the lemon rind and juice and mix well. Add this to the melted butter and sugar and continue cooking over boiling water /double boiler stirring continuously till thick and set. It should be of spreading consistency (like jam).

Final Assembly:

Butter a dish to fit the pancakes. Lay a pancake at the bottom of dish. Spread generously with Lemon Curd. Place another pancake on top. Spread with lemon curd and cover again with a pancake. Continue in this way till all the pancakes are finished. Do not spread Lemon curd on the top pancake. Also do not make this dessert too high. Chill for several hours. Next turn out on a flat dessert dish. Cover the whole with beaten cream. Chill once more. Before serving decorate with a little grated lemon rind. Serve with extra cream.

Variations

1. Instead of serving the above dish with extra fresh cream serve with a custard flavoured with lemon juice or make a lemon syrup with custard powder, sugar, and water instead of milk flavoured with lemon juice. Follow the instructions for making custard from the custard powder can or packet.

2. Substitute strawberry jam or whole strawberries and cream to sandwich the pancakes in place of Lemon Curd. Cover with cream and garnish with whole or sliced strawberries. This should be served with extra cream only.

3. Roll each pancake after spreading generously with Lemon Curd, Strawberry jam or Strawberries and cream. Lay side by side in a buttered rectangular dish. Make sure the pancakes are tightly packed. Cover thickly with well beaten double cream. Decorate with either grated lemon rind or sliced strawberries.

4. Peaches, (preferably canned), is another good substitute for the above dessert.

SOMLOI GALUSKA (A RICH CAKE DESSERT)

(This is most probably of Hungarian origin with a few variations. It makes a good party fare. This recipe was given to me by a good Hungarian friend. It might seem a very formidable recipe, but it is very easy to make. A simple but delicious dessert!)

9 eggs separated	10 oz. sugar
10 oz. flour	¾ tbsp. cocoa
3 oz. cashew or peanuts ground	

Method

Beat egg whites stiff. Add powdered sugar and beat some more. Stir in egg yolks and then add the flour. Divide dough into three parts. Add cocoa to one part and nuts to another part. Bake all three parts in a moderately hot oven for 15-20 minutes. Cool and keep aside.

Now sandwich the sponges with the following fillings.

First Filling:

12 oz. sugar	3 tblsp. water
2 tsp. rum or, cognac	1 tblsp. lemon rind grated

Mix all the above ingredients and cook for 10 minutes on medium heat. Keep aside to cool.

Second Filling:

5 oz. cashew or peanuts ground	3 oz. raisins
4 tblsp. heaped apricot or, mango jam	

Mix all the ingredients and keep aside

Third Filling:

10 oz. sugar	2½ tblsp. heaped cocoa

1 tblsp. water   1 tblsp. rum, or sherry

Cook above in a saucepan over medium heat for about 10 minutes. Cool and keep aside.

Place any one of the sponges on a platter. Spread the top with half of the 1st filling and then half of the 2nd. filling. Place a second sponge on top of this. Repeat the procedure with the leftovers of the first and second fillings. Cover with the third sponge. Spread with half of the 3rd. filling. Leave in the refrigerator for 1 or 2 days. Also store the leftover of the third filling in the refrigerator. After 1 or 2 days, take out cake from the refrigerator. Take off bits from the cake and place in a heap on a flat tray or platter till like a mound. Spread the rest of the third filling on the cake to cover. Decorate by covering with plenty of fresh beaten double cream. Sprinkle roasted and ground almonds on top and sides as garnish.

MOCHA DESSERT

1 lb. sponge cake round	3-4 eggs
1 cup fresh milk	1 cup sugar
1 cup thick fresh cream	½ cup soft butter
2 tblsp. cocoa	1 tblsp. strong coffee
A pinch of salt	¼ cup cognac or, any good brandy
Extra double cream for covering the dessert	4-5 cherries chopped

Method

Cut the sponge in 4 thin rounds for sandwiching. You will need only one round for the mocha dessert. (Sandwich the rest of the sponge with your favourite filling, dust with icing sugar, cut in serving pieces and serve or store for a later use.)

Butter a round mould and line with slices of the thin sponge kept aside. Make a thick custard with the egg, milk, and sugar. Cool. Mix the cream, butter, cocoa, coffee, salt, and brandy and beat all together till smooth. Make sure the butter is not too soft – just pliable. Add a bit of the sponge cake crumbled (to hold the dessert together) and mix well. Pile onto the sponge slices in the mould. Press down and chill. When well set un-mould on a flat dish. Cover with more thick cream, garnish with cherries and chill for a while before serving. This is an easy, rather rich dessert and can be made a day before use.

Variations

1. 1If the eggs are fresh and from a good source there is no need to make a custard. They can be added straight minus the milk but with the sugar to the rest of the ingredients and beaten.

2. Instead of lining the mould with sponge slices the sponge may be crumbled and added to the rest of the mixture and beaten. I always prefer this method.

BHAPA DOI OR BENGALI STEAMED YOGURT DESSERT (I)

½ pt. fresh milk	½ cup unsweetened, un-flavoured yogurt
¾ can condensed milk	1 tblsp. seedless raisins well washed
3-4 almonds blanched and grated	3-4 pistachios skinned and grated
1-2 sheets silver foil for garnish	

Method

Boil milk, turn heat down and let it simmer till quite thick for about ½ hour. Let it cool. In the meantime, mix yogurt and condensed milk till well blended. Add the thickened milk and once again blend all well till smooth and there are no lumps. Put mixture in an ovenproof greased dish. Sprinkle top with raisins, almonds, and pistachios. Put dish in a pan of water and then place it on the lowest shelf of the oven at the lowest temperature. Let it cook slowly for about 1½ hours or till set. Test by inserting a toothpick in the centre of the dessert which should come out dry. Cool in the refrigerator before serving. Garnish with silver foil.

Variation

1¼ pt. fresh milk, 1 can condensed milk, ¾ cup unsweetened yogurt ¾ cup cottage cheese well mashed. Treat the fresh milk as above. Proceed with the method given thereafter adding the cottage cheese. After blending, it is better to strain the whole mixture through a nylon mesh strainer or muslin to get a smooth texture. Place mixture in a microwave safe dish and microwave on the lowest level (power 10) for 40 minutes. Garnish with silver foil, raisins, and almond slivers. For the extra flavour, can add a pinch of saffron diluted in warm milk to the mixture.

BHAPA DOI (II)

1 cup yogurt

1 litre fresh milk

2-4 tblsp. fine sugar

Method

Strain yogurt till all water is drained out. This is best done by placing yogurt in a cheese cloth and hanging it from the faucet of the sink. Boil milk, lower heat, and thicken till reduced to about ½ litre. Add the sugar and mix well. Cool and then strain as the yogurt to get all creamy lumps out. Mix both well. Pour in a greased ovenproof dish and continue as Bhapa Doi (I). Raisins, almonds, pistachios, and silver foil are optional.

BHAPA DOI (III)

2 cups yogurt

24 oz. cottage cheese

1 litre milk reduced to half as above recipes

8 oz. sugar

Method

Blend all the above ingredients and continue as the previous recipes. Alternately, instead of placing this dish in the oven it can be made in a steamer or pressure cooker till dessert is set However, make sure it is not over cooked in which case it will become crumbly, and the water content will separate giving it a harsh cheesy taste.

Micro-waving in the lowest power is also a good option.

YOGURT TOFFEE OR BURFI OF BHAPA (IV)

1 litre milk	250 gm. unsweetened yogurt
125 gm. sugar	1 tsp. or less, almonds blanched and slivered
2 tblsp. raisins	½ tsp. seeds from a big brown cardamom
1 tsp. or less pistachio slivered	2-4 tsp. rose water according to taste

Method

Boil milk down to half the quantity. Beat yogurt till smooth and then mix with the milk and sugar. Pour mixture into a greased shallow ovenproof dish. Sprinkle top with the nuts, raisins, and cardamom. Cover bowl and steam by placing over a saucepan of hot water over medium to low heat. Should set in ½-1 hour. Do not overcook or else it will curdle losing the smoothness. When ready take off heat, cool, sprinkle with the rose water and decorate top with silver paper. Cut in square or diamond shapes.

BENGALI MISHTI DOI OR SWEET YOGURT (I)

2 cups milk	1 tblsp. white sugar
4 tblsp. water	2 tblsp. brown sugar
2 tsp. gelatine	1 tblsp. yogurt

Method

Bring the milk to boil on high heat and then reduce heat to medium and continue boiling the milk for another 5 minutes. stirring continuously scraping the bottom and the sides. Strain milk through a muslin or cheese cloth so that there are no lumps. Caramelise the white sugar with 2 tblsp. water. Return milk to medium heat. Add the caramelised sugar and stir to blend the milk and sugar. Take off heat. Add the brown sugar to the hot milk and mix well. Soak the gelatine in 2 tblsp water. Cook over warm water till gelatine is melted and clear. Add to the milk while both are still warm so that they blend quickly. There should be no lumps in the mixture. This can be ensured by gently beating the milk mixture with a rotary beater or a hand blender. When cool, add the yogurt and blend well to mix. Pour into a glass or enamel bowl. Put the bowl in another pan of hot water which should only come halfway up making sure the water does not enter the yogurt. Cover the yogurt preferably with a clean, thick cloth or tea towel. Place in a warm (not hot) place e.g. a cold oven or a large casserole flask with cover till set. This should take about 2-2½ hours depending on the climate.

MISHTI DOI (II)

2 cups milk

2 tblsp. plain yogurt

4-6 tblsp. condensed milk

Method

Bring milk to the boil on high heat. Reduce heat and simmer for 15 minutes or till milk is reduced to ¾ of the original amount. Cool. Beat in the condensed milk and yogurt. Make sure all well blended with no lumps. Cover and place in a warm place till set. Place in the refrigerator for a couple of hours or more before serving.

MOCK SHRIKHAND

Approximate Measurements

1 cup yogurt	4 tblsp. sugar
¼ tsp. saffron	1 tblsp. raisin
2 tsp. almond blanched and slivered	Rose petal/silver foil for garnish (optional)

Method

This is a good summer dessert especially if the yogurt is a day or two old and slightly fermented and not very palatable.

Place the yogurt in a soup strainer or muslin with a bowl or deep dish/saucepan underneath to hold the liquid which drips from it. Cover and keep in this manner for several hours throwing out the liquid from time to time. When all the liquid has been drained and the yogurt is fairly dry, put it in a blender with sugar to taste and a pinch or ¼ tsp saffron (depending on the amount of yogurt and preference for saffron). Blend the mixture on high speed till all well blended. Place in a dessert bowl, sprinkle top with raisins and blanched slivered almonds. Can also garnish with fresh clean rose petals or silver foil sheet. Chill before serving. If desired a few ground almonds may be blended with the yogurt to give it an "almondish" flavour. Reserve a few for sprinkling on top.

Variation: The above can also be made without straining the yogurt. Just discard the excess liquid if any. Next blend with 2 tblsp. sugar and 1 tsp. salt or to taste. 1 tsp. each freshly roasted and ground coriander and cumin seeds. Add 1-2 tblsp. fresh lemon juice for added flavour.

GINGER MARMALADE STEAM PUDDING

6 oz. sugar

3 eggs

1 tsp. baking powder

4 tblsp. heaped marmalade

6 oz. margarine or butter

6 oz. flour

1 tblsp. ginger powder

2 cups water

Method

Beat the sugar and butter till soft and fluffy. Add the eggs one at a time beating the mixture after each addition. Sift all the dry ingredients together and fold into the egg mixture. Pour into a greased and floured heat-proof pudding mould. Cover and steam in a double boiler or steamer or pressure cook for approximately ½ hour or till pudding is done. Un-moulded on a serving dish. Heat the marmalade and water to boiling and then simmer on low heat for about 5 minutes or till thick. Pour over the pudding. Serve pudding with fresh cream or custard.

STEAMED ORANGE PUDDING

6 oz. flour	1 tsp. heaped baking powder
4 oz. butter	4 oz. sugar
3-4 eggs	2 tsp. fresh orange rind finely grated
2 tsp. crystallized ginger grated	1-2 tblsp. top of milk

Method

Sift the flour and baking powder and keep aside. Cream butter and sugar. Beat and add the eggs one at a time. Next add the orange rind and ginger. Finally add the flour. Mix well. If the dough is too dry or stiff add sufficient top of milk to form a soft but not sticky dough. Grease and flour a heat proof round pudding bowl. Pour dough into the bowl and smoothen the top. Cover with a grease - proof paper so that no water goes into the bowl. Steam in the pressure cooker or steamer for about 45 minutes or 1 hour. till done. Test with a tooth - pick inserted in the centre. It should come out clean. Serve with custard and diluted orange honey. A very welcome dessert to end a winter dinner/supper.

<u>Orange Honey:</u>

Mix 2 tblsp orange honey and 1 tblsp water in a saucepan and bring to the boil. Remove from heat and serve.

Variations

1. Use 1 tsp ginger powder instead of crystallized ginger. Sift the ginger powder with the flour and baking powder.
2. If orange honey is not available use 2 tblsp plain honey with 1 tblsp fresh orange juice and 1 tblsp water. Continue as above.

Note

This pudding can also be cooked in the microwave for 5 minutes (more or less) or till done at power 7.

ORANGE SPONGE PUDDING

3 eggs separated	6 tblsp. powdered/castor sugar
8 tblsp. flour	1 tsp. baking powder
2 tsp. lemon/orange rind finely grated	4 tblsp. orange marmalade/orange honey
6 tblsp. water	

Method

Beat the egg whites stiff. Add the sugar gradually and keep on beating. Next add the egg yolks one at a time beating after each addition. Sift the flour, baking powder and the grated lemon or orange rind and then gently fold into the egg mixture. Make sure the batter is smooth and not lumpy. Turn into a preferably a non-stick cake pan and bake in a moderate oven for about $\frac{1}{2}$ hour or till done. Mix marmalade or honey with the water and heat in a saucepan. Let it come to a boil and then simmer for 3-4 minutes. Pour over the cake while still warm. Serve with custard or cream. If desired extra orange sauce can be made and served separately along with the custard.

BAKED GUAVA PUDDING

2 cups guava pulp

1½ cups milk

1 tsp. vanilla essence

¼ tsp. cinnamon powder

4 tblsp. sugar

3-4 eggs

¼ tsp. nutmeg

Method

Mix and beat all the ingredients together till well blended. Pour in a greased pudding bowl. Place bowl in a pan of water and bake in a moderately hot oven till done. Test doneness by inserting a skewer or fork in the centre of the pudding. If the skewer comes out clean and dry the pudding is done. Cool and then unmould on a flat dish. Pour guava syrup over it and serve with fresh cream or custard.

<u>Guava Syrup:</u>

4 tblsp. guava jelly   1 cup water

Mix the above and bring to a boil. Lower heat and simmer for about 3-4 minutes. Pour over pudding while still warm.

STEAMED GUAVA OR FRUIT PUDDING

Dough:

4 oz. lard or, any other fat   8 oz. flour

Ice water as required

Filling:

250 gm. guava pulp   4 tblsp. sugar

1 tblsp. lemon juice   2 tblsp. flour/corn flour

Method

Mix all the filling ingredients together and keep aside till required.

For the dough -- cut the fat into the flour and mix quickly to resemble breadcrumbs. Add enough ice water little at a time to form a soft pliable dough – it should not be too soggy or too dry. Form dough into a ball, cover and store in the refrigerator till required.

Grease and flour a heat - proof bowl. Take dough out of the refrigerator. Pat with rolling pin to flatten and then roll out to fit the bowl with enough dough hanging over the sides to cover pudding later. Place filling inside the dough and cover carefully with the extra dough that is hanging over the sides. (Alternately place filling in the bowl and cover only the top with the dough pulling a little to cover the edge and sealing it.) Pressure cook for approximately 20 minutes – ½ hour. Open pressure cooker when cool and turn over on a flat dish. If dough is used only to cover the top of the pudding, then serve in the bowl. Serve with honey sauce – 2 tblsp honey and 4 tblsp water heated together poured over the pudding. Cream or custard should be served as an accompaniment separately.

Variation:

1. Substitute apple or pineapple or a mixture of any fruits instead of guava. A handful of raisins can be added.

2. Use brown sugar in place of white sugar and flavour with any of the following powders: ¼ tsp of cinnamon, clove, nutmeg, mace, a combination of any of the spices or mixed spice.

3. Instead of steaming the dessert, it can be baked on a medium oven for 20-30 minutes or, till the pastry is a golden-brown colour.

GUAVA KHEER

2 litre full cream milk

1 tsp. saffron soaked in 1 tblsp. warm milk

Silver paper/rose petals for garnish

2 lbs. ripe guavas peeled

2-4 tblsp. condensed milk/1 cup cream (optional)

1 cup powdered castor sugar (more or less)

Method

Boil the milk down in a heavy bottomed saucepan to 1 liter, stirring continuously and scraping the sides and bottom. Do not let the milk burn at the bottom. Keep aside to cool. Purée the guava pulp, strain to remove the seeds if any. Stir guava into the cooled milk. Return to very low heat and cook for 5-10 minutes stirring continuously. The mixture should not curdle. Take off heat and cool. Add the saffron, condensed milk or cream (if using) for added flavour. Now add as much sugar as required. Stir all gently to blend. Pour into a dessert bowl and refrigerate. Let it settle a little. Garnish with silver paper or a sprinkling of fresh pink rose petals washed properly. This dessert should not be too thick or too thin.

SIMPLE BREAD PUDDING

4 oz. granulated sugar

½ litre fresh milk

1 tblsp. raisins

1 tblsp. orange peel finely slivered

4 eggs separated

1 oz. castor sugar

4 tblsp. water

4 oz. bread (without crust) crumbled

1 tblsp. cherries chopped

1 tblsp. crystallized ginger finely slivered or 1-2 tsp. ginger powder

2 tblsp. sherry/rum/brandy/any liqueur

Method

Caramelize the granulated sugar and water. Take off heat and cool. Add the milk and cook on low heat till caramel and milk well blended. Do not let the mixture boil. Pour mixture over the crumbled bread and let soak for about ½ hour. Add the raisins, cherries, orange peel, ginger, sherry, beaten egg yolks, castor sugar and mix well. Last of all beat the egg whites stiff and fold into the bread mixture stirring gently to blend lightly. Pour mixture in a well buttered oven proof dish.

Put the dish on a baking tray with water which should come quarter up the main dish. Bake in a moderate hot oven and bake for about 1 hour. or till set. Test doneness by inserting a skewer in the middle which should come out clean and not soggy. Serve hot with sherry (or any other flavouring used) flavoured fresh cream or custard.

RIKI'S BREAD PUDDING

6-8 cups white bread (not too fresh) crumbled

4 cups milk or, ½ milk and ½ heavy cream

2 cups sugar

8 tblsp. butter melted

3 eggs

2-4 tblsp. vanilla essence

1 tsp. cinnamon powder

½ tsp. nutmeg powder

3-5 cups dry fruits diced small (raisins, nuts, coconuts, cherries etc.)

Method

Combine all the above ingredients till well mixed. The mixture should be moist but not soupy. Pour into a buttered 9"×9" baking dish and bake in a moderate oven for about 1 hr.15 minutes till top is golden brown. Serve with the following whisky sauce.

<u>Whisky Sauce:</u>

¼ lb butter

1½ cup sugar powdered

1 whole egg or, only yolk

½ cup whisky/any other alcohol or substitute/one-third cup whisky + one third cup orange juice

Cream butter and sugar over low heat until blended but not caramelised. Remove from heat and blend in the whole egg or just the yolk. Pour in the alcohol or substitute, mix well and return to low heat. Stir continuously till the sauce thickens.

CHOCOLATE BREAD PUDDING

8 oz. bread crumbled	1¼ cup fresh milk
4 tblsp. sugar	1 tblsp. cocoa powder
1 tsp. vanilla essence	4 egg yolks
1 tblsp. butter melted	1 tblsp. rum or brandy
4 egg whites	¼ tsp. cream of tartar
1 tblsp. icing sugar	2-3 cherries grated or chopped for garnish

Method

Soak the crumbled bread in just enough milk to cover. Rest till it becomes soggy. Warm the milk with the sugar and cocoa till sugar dissolves. Add the vanilla essence. Take off heat and let cool slightly. Beat in the egg yolks making sure the milk does not curdle. Add the bread and butter. Mix well till mixture is smooth. There should be no lumps. Add the rum or brandy and stir well to mix evenly. Put the mixture into a well-greased oven proof pudding dish. Smoothen top. Beat the egg whites with the cream of tartar. Add the icing sugar at the last minute. Spread evenly on the pudding. Bake in a moderate oven for 15–20 minutes till set and the meringue has browned. Just before taking out of the oven, sprinkle with the grated cherries- optional. Serve with vanilla ice cream or plain fresh cream.

Variation:

1. Instead of adding the egg yolks after dissolving the sugar with the milk and cocoa, combine the cold milk, egg yolks, sugar, and cocoa in a saucepan. Cook on low heat stirring continuously till it thickens like a custard. The custard may also be made in a double boiler. Add the vanilla essence just before taking off the heat. Now continue as above.

2. **Orange Bread Pudding:** Make this exactly like the chocolate bread pudding but omit the cocoa and vanilla. Instead, when the custard has cooled and mixed with the bread and butter add the strained juice of 2 large oranges or 4 tblsp. fresh orange juice and 1 tblsp. finely grated orange rind. Rum or brandy should also be added at this time. Follow the steps as in chocolate bread pudding. Serve with fresh cream.

PLUM DUMPLING

½ litre milk

300 gm. flour or 75 gm. semolina + 225 gm. flour

2 eggs

A pinch of salt

100 gm. butter or any fat

10-12 (more or less) red plums

Breadcrumbs, butter, and icing sugar for sprinkling on top of dumplings

Method

Bring milk and butter to the boil. Next add the flour, mix and keep stirring till dough is stiff and very hard. Take off heat and cool. Sprinkle a board with flour and spread dough. When cold add the eggs and salt by placing them in the centre of the dough. Knead dough well adding enough flour if required. Shape dough into a long thin roll like a sausage. Cut off small portions from the dough the size of a demitasse saucer. Place a plum in the centre of each piece of cut dough. Pull up dough to cover plum and shape into a ball. Rest the plum balls for 6-8 hours. Just before serving boil the balls in salted water in a covered pot. Make sure the water reaches post boiling stage before putting the plum balls in. These balls can be refrigerated for a long time and boiled just before needed.

Fry breadcrumbs in butter a little till red, then roll the plum dumplings in this mixture. Alternately sprinkle fried breadcrumbs over the plum dumplings. Next, sprinkle icing sugar and serve. This is good as a mid-morning coffee or tea-time snack, or a dessert served with clotted or plain cream.

Variations

Instead of fresh plums canned plums may be substituted. In this case strain plums well. Instead of breadcrumbs grated cream or cottage cheese may also be used.

BAKED OR PRESSURE-COOKED STUFFED APPLES

2-4 apples required depending on the number of guests

Per Apple:

1 tsp. butter	1 tsp brown sugar
1 tsp. raisins	A pinch of cinnamon powder

Method

Core apple without making a hole right through. Mix all the above ingredients and fill the opening of the apple pressing down slightly. Place on a baking tray and bake in a moderate oven for 10–15 minutes or till apples are soft but not soggy. Serve hot on individual plates with cream or custard. If pressure cooking place stuffed apple in another shallow bowl or dish to avoid water splashing it. The apple may be covered with foil for further protection. Pressure cook for about 3-5 minutes. Let the pressure drop by itself before opening the cooker.

Variation

The stuffed apple is equally good steamed in a double boiler, steamer, or rice cooker.

MANGO SURPRISE

1 sponge cake from 3 eggs	½ cup (more or less) rum
4 good, ripe mangoes peeled, sliced, and mashed	1 tsp. vanilla essence
A few slices of mango for decoration	3 cups fresh cream

Method

Slice and crumble cake and soak in the rum for ½ hour. Add the mango pulp, vanilla essence and 2 cups cream. Blend all together preferably in a food processor to get a smooth texture. Wet the inside of a round pudding bowl with cold water – best done by holding it under a running cold-water tap. Shake off all excess water but do not dry. Fill bowl with the mango mixture, cover and chill in the refrigerator for several hours preferably overnight. Invert bowl on a flat dish and gently tap the top and sides to un-mould the dessert. Beat 1 cup cream stiff and cover dessert completely. Decorate with slices of mango and chill for another 1-2 hours before serving.

Variation

1. Mango may be substituted with any other fruit e.g. strawberries, peaches, apricots, blueberries etc.
2. Instead of crumbling the sponge cake divide into 3-4 layers and sandwich with mango or any other fruit slices or pulp and cream. Cover the cake with beaten cream and decorate with the fruit being used.

MANGO OR FRUIT FLAN

1/8" thin round baked short-crust pastry

1" thick round sponge cake

1-2 (more or less) mango sliced

2 tblsp. water/fruit juice

1 tblsp. or less, any jam

2 tblsp. more or less rum/fruit juice

1 tblsp. gelatine powder

2-4 tblsp. cream/vanilla custard

Method

Place short crust pastry at the base of an 8"-9" round flat dish. Spread lightly with some jam. Place sponge on top and gently press down. Sprinkle the rum or juice liberally over the sponge. Now arrange the mango slices cut in crescents in a nice pattern on the sponge till covered. Dissolve the gelatine in the water/fruit juice over a bowl of hot water stirring continuously. Pour this over evenly on the fruit and cake to give a glaze. Spread cream/custard over the glaze. Refrigerate for several hours till well set. Serve with thick fresh cream or custard.

ORANGE FLAN

1 cup orange juice	2 tblsp. Rum (optional)
2 tblsp. orange honey, marmalade or, jam	3 oranges peeled and segmented
2 egg whites beaten stiff	½ cup fresh cream beaten
2 tblsp icing sugar	2 tsp. gelatine
½ cup water	Biscuit dough as below
Sponge cake as below	

Method

Soak the two sponge halves with the orange juice and rum. Spread the top of the biscuit dough with honey or substitute. Place the sponge cakes on top of each dough. Spread the entire surface of both the cakes with whole or halved orange segments. Mix the beaten egg whites, cream and sugar and pour over the orange segments. Soak gelatine in the water and heat over hot water to melt and form a clear glaze. Pour over cream mixture evenly. Refrigerate for 2-3 hours or till set. Cut in slices and serve with tea or coffee or as a dessert with extra cream. Makes 2 flans.

Biscuit Dough:

4 oz. flour	2 oz. butter or margarine
2 egg yolks	1-2 tblsp. (approx.) milk

Mix flour and butter till resembles breadcrumbs. Add the yolks stirring with a wooden spoon. Add sufficient milk, only, if necessary, to bind dough. Divide dough into two portions and roll into ¼" thick rounds of 6" diameter. Place on an oiled and floured baking tray. Prick surface of dough with a fork. Bake in a moderate oven till pastry is a light brown or as soon as crust is hard to the touch. Do not over bake.

Sponge Cake:

2 eggs separated	3 tblsp. castor sugar
4 tblsp. flour	1 tsp. baking powder
1 tsp. grated orange rind	

Beat egg whites stiff. Add the sugar gradually and continue beating. Add yolks one at a time beating after each addition. Sift flour with the baking powder and add to the egg mixture. Stir in the grated rind. Fold in the egg whites. Pour mixture into a greased and floured round cake pan of 6" diameter. Bake in a medium hot oven for 45 minutes or till done. Cool on a wire tray. Divide sponge into two rounds equally.

Variation

Other fruits such as mangoes, peaches, plums etc can be substituted for oranges. Soak sponge with rum or brandy or any juice that will blend with the fruit used. The egg whites may be omitted especially if the cream is thick.

ORANGE CUPS

1 doz. sweet oranges

4 oz. sugar

1 tsp. vanilla essence

2 tblsp. or more rum (optional)

Fresh double/heavy cream as required (optional)

1 pt. milk

4 eggs separated

2 tblsp. gelatine powder

¼ tsp. edible orange colouring (optional)

2-4 tsp. orange rind grated fine

Method

Cut oranges in half and squeeze out the juice without damaging the outer casing or cups. Reserve the cups. Mix milk, sugar and egg yolks thoroughly and then cook on top of the stove stirring continuously with a wooden spoon to make a thick custard. Take off heat and cool. Add the vanilla essence. Dissolve the gelatine in 2-4 tblsp. warm orange juice – there should not be any lumps. Add this to the rest of the orange juice and mix well till smooth. Add the rum if using. Stir the juice gradually to the custard and blend in well. Add the orange colouring, if using. Beat the egg whites stiff and then gradually fold into the custard. Add 1 tsp grated orange rind. Divide the mixture into the 24 half orange cups. Spread the top of each with cream or make a swirling design with the cream. Refrigerate till dessert is set. Before serving, sprinkle with orange rind.

ORANGE CREAM

Sponge Cake:

4 oz. butter	4 oz. castor sugar
2 eggs separated	4 oz. flour
½ tsp. baking powder	2 tblsp. milk (more or less)

Biscuit Dough:

4 oz. flour	A pinch of salt
2 oz. sugar	2 oz. butter/margarine

Orange Cream:

1-2 cups orange juice (more or less)	2-3 tblsp. butter/margarine
3-4 tblsp. thick cream/mock cream	1-2 tblsp. rum/sherry/brandy (optional)
2 oranges cut into segments with seeds and thread removed	

Method

Make a sponge cake by mixing the butter and sugar together. Add the yolks one at a time gently beating after each addition to blend. Sift flour and baking powder together. Add flour to the butter mixture gradually and keep stirring with a wooden spoon until well blended. If mixture is too dry only then add sufficient milk to get a cake consistency keeping in mind the addition of the egg whites to come. Beat the egg whites stiff and gently fold into the sponge mixture. Turn into a greased cake tin and bake in a moderate oven 30-45 minutes. When cool cut up roughly and keep aside.

Make the biscuit dough by sifting the flour, salt, and sugar. Add the softened butter and mix. Roll out into a large round or rectangle about ¼"in thickness. Place in a greased and floured baking tray and bake in a moderate oven for 15-20 mins or till golden brown and ready. Cool and break roughly.

It is better to make the sponge and the biscuit dough a day ahead. Now put the sponge and biscuit in the food processor. Process until like fine breadcrumbs. Add enough orange juice from the orange cream to moisten. Next add the butter/margarine, cream and alcohol if using. Process till all well blended. Finally add some of the orange segments and process a couple of seconds to mix. It does not matter if some of the orange segments do not blend well with the rest of the mixture. Line the bottom and sides of a mould with orange segments. Pour the mixture into the mould. Refrigerate for several hours. Before serving turn out onto a flat dish and decorate with a sprinkling of orange zest.

COTTAGE CHEESE DESSERT

2 lbs. cottage cheese	8 oz. sugar
3-4 eggs	2-4 tblsp. condensed milk
1 tsp. saffron diluted in 2 tblsp. warm milk	1-2 tblsp. raisins
1 tblsp. almond slivers	2 tsp. pistachio slivers

Method

Put the cottage cheese and sugar in the food processor to blend evenly. Add the eggs and condensed milk and continue to process. Lastly add the saffron and process for a couple of seconds. Turn into a greased oven proof dessert dish. Sprinkle top with the raisins, almonds, and pistachios. Place dish in a pan of water. The water should be just below the halfway mark of the dessert dish. It should not spill into the dish while cooking. Bake in a moderate oven for 15-20 minutes. Insert a toothpick in the centre of the dessert which should come out clean as in a cake. Leave in the dish or turn out on a flat dish. In the latter case, sprinkle the raisins, almonds, and pistachios at the bottom of the dish and then pour the cottage cheese mixture over it before baking. Refrigerate when ready, till required.

Variations

(to serve this simple but delicious dessert):

1. Garnish top of dessert with silver paper after dessert has been cooled. Serve with cream, "*rabri*" (thickened milk) or 4-6 tblsp condensed milk mixed with 1-1½ cup water which should again be slightly thickened.

2. When dessert is cool pour 1-2 tblsp honey or "*nolen gur*" (liquid date palm jaggery) directly on top of the dessert. Alternately the honey/*nolen gur* can be diluted with a little water and then heated and served like an accompanying sauce. A cinnamon stick can be added to the liquid during the heating process, but it should be removed before serving.

LEFT-OVER FROZEN DESSERT

¼ lb. or more stale chocolate cake

1 tub. left over vanilla ice cream

1 tblsp. rum/sherry/brandy or any other liqueur

2-4 tblsp. double cream for covering dessert

2 tblsp. cherries chopped for garnishing

2 tsp. almonds chopped for garnishing

Method

Put cake and ice-cream in a food processor and process till well blended. Add the flavouring. Rinse a round mould in cold water. Pour mixture into it, cover with foil and freeze. Just before serving turn out on a flat dish, cover completely with cream and decorate with the cherries and almonds.

AMBROSIA

(This is a quick, delicious, inexpensive recipe which can be made from left over sponge cake and fruits from other recipes.)

¼-½ cup fruit syrup	½ lb. (more or less) sponge cake crumbled
1 cup (more or less) fruit chopped	1 tblsp. gelatine
2-4 tblsp. fresh cream (optional)	2-4 tblsp. cold water
2-4 tblsp. rum, brandy, or sherry	

Method

Add the fruit syrup to the crumbled cake till soft and a little mushy. Add the chopped fruit – preferably canned fruit and mix gently. Dissolve the gelatine in the water and then add to the cake mixture. Next add the cream if using and the rum. Blend all lightly till smooth. Put in a mould and place in the refrigerator to set for 1-2 hrs. or more. Un-mould just before serving on a flat dish. Garnish with more fruit and serve with whipped fresh cream.

BOMBÉ ALASKA

1 thin round or square slice of sponge cake cut horizontally from a 2 lb. sponge cake,

Or 1 lb. sponge cake baked in a 2 lb. tin

1-2 tblsp. jam of any flavour or, raisins and/or chopped walnuts and almonds

2 egg whites beaten stiff

1-2 tblsp. (or more) sherry, cognac, or rum

½-1 kg. brick plain vanilla ice cream moulded into the same shape as the sponge

4 oz. castor sugar

Method

Sprinkle sponge with the liquor. Spread with jam or raisins and nuts. Put ice cream on this in a mound. The ice cream should not go out of the periphery of the sponge. Beat egg whites stiff. Fold in the sugar. Cover cake and ice cream completely with the meringue. If necessary, use more egg whites and sugar. Not too much of the latter or else the Alaska will be too sweet. This can be prepared in advance and stored in the deep freeze. Just before serving pre-heat the oven to 400^0 F. Place the Alaska carefully in the hot oven for about 4-5 minutes or till meringue is gently browned.

While assembling the Alaska put it in the deep freeze if ice cream is too runny before covering with meringue. Can decorate the meringue with cherries, nuts, or raisins before placing the Alaska in the oven.

ICE CREAMS

BASIC ICE CREAM

500 gm. evaporated milk, or ½ condensed milk and ½ water, or 1 litre milk boiled down to ½ litre

2 tsp. heaped gelatine

1-2 tblsp. heaped sugar (omit sugar if condensed milk is used

2 tblsp. water

1 tsp. vanilla essence or, substitute

2 tblsp. powdered milk

Method

Chill for a while whatever milk is being used. Dissolve gelatine in water. Beat milk and sugar until stiff. In the case of condensed milk, beat without sugar. Fold in whatever essence or flavouring is being used. Add the dissolved gelatine and mix well. Pour in a cold container and set in the deep freeze. When set, take out and beat once adding a little (approx. 2 tblsp) powdered milk so that the ice cream is not crunchy. Put back in the freezer compartment.

SIMPLE ICE CREAM

2 cups condensed milk

Add any flavouring

Ground almonds or walnuts

1 cup (or a little more) fresh cream

Marsala wine

Ice cream wafers

Method

Beat condensed milk, cream and flavouring altogether and freeze. Serve in individual bowls with a scoop. Top each with 1 tsp. of wine. Sprinkle with nuts. Stick a wafer at a jaunty angle!

Variation

In the absence of marsala wine, cognac or sherry may be used. Another good substitute is "*Nolen Gur*". This is a liquid *jaggery* from date palm available usually in the winter in Bengal.

VANILLA ICE CREAM

½ litre milk

2 tsp. vanilla essence

1 tblsp. corn flour

5 tblsp. heaped crystal sugar

1-2 egg yolks

½ cup fresh cream

Method

Bring to boil three quarters of milk with sugar and vanilla. Lower heat and simmer for 10 minutes. Keep stirring from time to time. Mix egg yolks, corn flour and the rest of the milk till smooth. Add to the above mixture stirring continuously till well blended and no lumps appear. Take off heat, place in a dish of cold water and keep stirring. When cool put in ice cream tray and freeze. When well set, take out and blend in fresh cream. Re-freeze covered till required. The texture should be smooth and soft. It should not be iced over

----

CHOCOLATE ICE CREAM

½ litre milk

½ tblsp. heaped crystal sugar

1 egg yolk

½ cup fresh cream

½ tblsp. corn flour or, 5 tblsp. grated chocolate

1 tblsp. cocoa

Method

Make chocolate ice cream as like the Vanilla Ice cream. If using cocoa, mix with the flour and sift. If using grated chocolate then cook with the milk during the first stage, so that it melts easily and blends in well with all the ingredients.

LEMON ICE CREAM

½ litre milk

1 tblsp. corn flour

2 tblsp. lemon juice

6 tblsp. heaped sugar

2 egg yolks

½ cup fresh cream

Method

Bring ¾ of the milk and sugar to boil. Lower heat for about 5 minutes. Mix the rest of the milk with the flour and yolks well and add to the above mixture. Keep stirring till well blended. Take off heat and place in a dish of cold water and keep stirring. When cold add the lemon juice and freeze. Make sure the mixture is cool before adding the lemon juice otherwise the milk will curdle. When the ice cream is set, take out and add fresh cream and re-set in the freezer.

ORANGE OR ANY OTHER FRUIT ICE CREAM

Method

To the basic ice-cream, just before freezing stir in orange segments or any other bits of fruit with a flavour. Fruits may be substituted with bits of chocolate or just chocolate chips.

MANGO ICE CREAM

Method

Follow the same method as the jackfruit ice cream. If the mangoes are too sweet either cut down on mango pulp or reduce the sugar quantity. Just before serving add small bits of mango pieces and stir gently to mix. When serving, garnish top with 1-2 slivers of mango if desired.

STRAWBERRY ICE CREAM

Method

Follow the same method as the jackfruit and mango ice creams. However, the strawberries need not be made into a pulp. Instead cut them into very small bits and add to the egg and milk mixture. Garnish with chopped strawberries or sprinkle top with crumbled pink macaroon with a whole strawberry in the centre. If strawberries are not readily available substitute with 1-2 tsp strawberry essence / 1-2 tblsp strawberry syrup / 2-4 tblsp strawberry jam. Reduce the sugar if necessary. Canned strawberries may also be used for the mixture and the garnish. A squirt of strawberry syrup or sprinkle of strawberry jam can be used as garnish.

JACK FRUIT ICE CREAM

8 egg yolks

6-8 oz. sugar

1 lb. ripe jackfruit pulp

6-8 tblsp. cold water

1 litre milk

1 cup cream or, 2 tblsp. milk powder

Method

Mix the yolks with the water. Add the sugar and beat till well dissolved. Bring the milk to the boil, lower heat and simmer for 5 minutes stirring frequently and scraping the sides. Cool milk, add to the egg and stir to blend well. Now add the jackfruit pulp and again stir to mix well. Cook mixture on low heat stirring continuously till it begins to thicken. Do not let it curdle. Take off heat and cool. Put in an ice cream machine till done. When the ice cream is ready, store in the freezer if not serving immediately. In the absence of an ice cream machine put the mixture in a container and freeze. After ½ hour to 45 minutes take the ice cream out of the freezer and beat in the cream or the milk powder made into a paste with a little fresh milk. Reset covered in the freezer. Serve as and when needed in ice-cream bowls or cups decorated with wafers.

PEPPERMINT ICE CREAM

Method

Use any of the above ice cream recipes. Flavour with 1-2 tblsp green creme de menthe. 1 tblsp ground peppermint or mint lozenges may be used with the original mixture. A drop of green colouring can be used if desired. Serve with Hot Fudge or Chocolate Sauce.

Hot Fudge or Chocolate Sauce

2 cups sugar	2 oz. unsweetened chocolate
A dash of salt	1 tblsp. butter
¾ cup evaporated milk or, ¼ cup condensed milk, or ½ cup fresh full cream milk	½ tsp. vanilla

If using condensed milk lessen the quantity of sugar by ½ cup or a little more. Sweetened chocolate may also be used in which case again reduce the sugar by ½ cup or more.

Combine all ingredients except vanilla in a saucepan. Cook on low heat till sugar and chocolate is melted. Now cook on medium heat and let boil till the contents form a soft ball stage or becomes a fairly set thick mass. Do not let it harden. Always use a wooden spoon. Remove from heat, add vanilla. Serve with the above ice cream.

PEANUT ICE CREAM

(I got the idea of this ice cream as a kid from my father. This was his specialty and contribution to the culinary accomplishments of his wife, my mother, and his mother-in-law, my grandmother. He usually ventured towards making peanut ice cream when my mother was away from home for long periods, and he was left to fend for his two older daughters – the younger two always got to accompany my mother! This was always a hot favourite with all his young nephews who were regular visitors to the house during my mother's absence. I now suspect it was the lure of the Peanut Ice Cream!!

Chopped peanuts were probably used in my father's recipe. I remember coming across quite a bit of peanut skin flakes which actually added to the flavour as the peanuts were roasted before being added to the ice cream mixture. I can still taste the delicious smoky, peanutty ice *cream*.

However, to make life a little less complicated I give below my easy version of the Peanut Ice Cream.)

Method

Add ¼-½ cup peanut butter to any of the ice creams above. Garnish scoops of ice cream with a sprinkling of finely chopped peanuts. I would recommend homemade peanut butter with a few roughly chopped peanuts thrown in for that extra crunchy touch.

Variations

Mango Ice Cream: Use ½ -1 cup canned mango pulp or mango juice or mashed fresh good quality mango. Bits of chopped mango may be mixed with the ice cream just before freezing.

Peach, Strawberry, Passion Fruit, Orange, Lemon, or any other fruit with flavour may be used to make ice cream as above. However, in the case of Lemon use just 1-2 tblsp of the juice.

PATALI (SOLID DATE JAGGERY) ICE CREAM

(Patali Goor, or solid date jaggery, is a speciality of Bengal available mainly during the winter months. However, now it is often available throughout the year also and in other parts of India such as New Delhi. Since patali is sweet sugar can safely be omitted.)

4-6 tblsp. water	4-6 egg yolks
8 oz. *patali* grated and mashed	1 litre milk
1-2 tsp. ginger powder	1 cup fresh cream
2 tblsp. powdered milk	1 tsp. sweet red wine

Method

Stir the water into the yolks till blended. Now mix this with the *patali* and beat till light. Beat in the cold milk gradually. Add the ginger powder and stir to mix. Cook in a double boiler or over a pan of hot water stirring continuously till mixture is thick. Do not let the mixture boil or it will curdle. Put in an ice-cream machine if available or else put in a cold container with a tight lid and place in the freezer compartment till half set. Beat the ice-cream and fold in the cream. At this time add powdered milk to the ice-cream to get a smooth texture and prevent it from getting crunchy. Return to the freezer compartment till required   Serve sprinkled with a little sweet red wine.

ROSOMALAI ICE CREAM

(*Rosomalai* is a very popular Indian dessert which can be bought in most Indian sweet shops or made at home. It is basically cottage cheese balls – "rosogollas" - in thickened milk. In North India the rosomalai rosogollas are much larger and the milk custard thinner than in Eastern India where the rosogollas are much smaller in very thickened milk.)

Method

This ice cream is made from left over rosomalai. When the rosomalai has been left in the refrigerator for a while the rosogollas often begin to crumble. Gently stir the rosomalai with a spoon and then place in the freezer compartment. Use an ice cream scoop for serving and garnish each scoop with slivers of pistachio and almonds and cover with silver paper.

MOCK ICE CREAM

1 litre milk

2-4 tblsp. condensed milk

2 tblsp. sugar

Any leftover Indian sweet e.g. *sandesh*, *rajbhog* etc.

Method

Boil milk down to ½ liter. Stir in the sugar and condensed milk and beat to blend well. Next break up and add the Indian sweets and again beat to blend well. If the sweets are not too highly flavoured add a pinch of saffron or ¼-½ tsp rose or *kewra* water. Put in the freezer compartment till set. The sugar and condensed milk may be reduced or increased depending on the amount of left over sweets being added. Place a small rose petal on top of each ice cream scoop as an added effect.

EGGLESS ICE CREAM

1 litre milk

4-5 tblsp. corn flour

1 cup cream – fresh/canned

6-8 tblsp. sugar

1-2 tsp. any flavouring essence or Liqueur

Method

Bring milk to the boil. Reduce heat to medium and add the sugar and keep stirring till the sugar dissolves. Reduce heat further to low. Mix the cornflour with a little cold water to make a paste. Add to the milk and stir continuously till the milk thickens. Take off heat and add any flavouring essence OR liqueur and then leave to cool. Add cream at this juncture if using. Put in an ice-cream machine. When ice-cream is ready store in a container with a lid and freeze till required. To get a smoother consistency and less crunchy take ice-cream out two or three times and beat thoroughly. Return to container till required. Beat once more an hour before serving Garnish top of each serving with a whirl of the liqueur used, or the fruit of the essence used.

Variations

1. **Cocoa/Coffee Ice Cream:** Use the same method as above but replace cornflour with custard powder. At the same time add 2 tblsp cocoa or 2 tblsp any instant coffee powder. Omit the flavouring essences but use an appropriate liqueur if desired. Garnish top of each serving by sprinkling grated chocolate

2. **Fruit Ice Cream:** Prepare basic ice-cream as above and then add small chunks of fruit e.g. melon, orange, grapefruit, mango etc.

3. **Patali or Date Palm Jaggery Ice Cream:** Add grated patali instead of sugar. Sprinkle the top of each serving with grated patali.

MANGO KULFI (INDIAN EGGLESS MANGO ICE CREAM)

2 litre milk

4 tblsp. corn flour

8 oz. fresh or canned cream (kept in the refrigerator till needed)

12 oz. sugar

3 large ripe mangoes puréed

Method

Bring milk to the boil and continue boiling for 2-3 minutes making sure it does not boil over by stirring continuously with a wooden spoon. Reduce heat and add the sugar. Simmer till sugar dissolves – approximately 10-15 minutes. Add the corn flour after mixing it with a little cold milk, stirring continuously to prevent lumps from forming. Blend well to form a pouring consistency. Take off heat and let cool. Take cream out of the refrigerator and blend with the mango purée. Add this to the cooled milk. Mix gently till all well blended and smooth. Pour into *kulfi* moulds ¾ full and freeze till required. Alternately pour into ice-cream trays or containers, cover and freeze.

CAKES

FLOATING ISLAND (CAKE)

3 eggs

8 heaped tblsp. flour

½ tsp. baking powder

9 tblsp. icing sugar

6 tblsp. water

Method

Separate egg yolks. Beat with sugar and water. Beat egg white stiff. Sift flour and baking powder. Fold in yolk mixture and blend well. Lastly fold in beaten egg whites and mix well. Bake in greased rectangular oven proof dish in a moderate oven for about 10 minutes or till done. When ready, cool, and then split in the middle and sandwich with jam – raspberry, strawberry, apricot etc. Now cut in small squares. Keep aside.

Vanilla Cream:

2 egg yolks

2 tsp. vanilla essence

2 heaped tblsp. corn flour

4 heaped tblsp. crystal sugar

2 cups milk

Mix yolks and sugar over very low heat. Gradually add milk and vanilla. Last of all fold in the flour very gently stirring continuously to avoid forming any lumps. Bring to boil and take off fire but keep on stirring for a while till a little cool. In a desert bowl lay the cake squares and vanilla cream alternately. The top layer should finish with the cream. Spread meringue on top of mixture and refrigerate till required.

Meringue:

2 egg whites beaten stiff

2 tblsp. castor sugar

2 or 3 tblsp. any jam or, melted chocolate

Mix all the above. This can be done in a blender or food processor. Brown meringue, under the grill just before serving or prior to refrigerating.

Note: This can also be served as a dessert.

SEMBE (MAIZE) CAKE (TANZANIA)

8 oz. butter

8 oz. sugar

5 large eggs

8 oz. maize flour

2 tsp. heaped baking powder

Method

Beat butter and sugar till well blended. Add egg one at a time and continue beating. Sift flour and baking powder and add to the above mixture. Grease and flour a round or square 8" cake tin. Pour in batter. Bake in a moderate oven (350^0F) for approximately 35 minutes. Do not overcook. On the other hand, do not under cook either. Test by inserting a skewer in the middle of the cake. It should come out clean and dry. This cake should have an even golden-brown colour.

POUND CAKE

Method

Use the same ingredients and method as above, making the following changes. Use self-raising white flour instead of maize flour. Omit the baking powder. However, if using non-self-rising flour then include the baking powder. Use 4 tblsp. heaped evaporated milk, or 1 heaped tblsp condensed milk and 4 tblsp milk or 8 tblsp full cream milk. Add the milk after the eggs. Continue as the maize cake.

MARBLE CAKE

4 oz. butter	5 oz. sugar
1 tsp. vanilla, almond or rum essence	2 eggs
8 oz. flour	1½ tsp. baking powder
A pinch of salt	6 oz. milk
2 oz. cocoa	Icing sugar

Method

Beat butter and 4 oz. of sugar together. Add essence of your choice – almond is recommended. Next add the eggs and mix all thoroughly. Sift together flour, baking powder and salt. Add to the butter mixture a little-by-little alternating with only 4 oz. of milk.

Grease and flour a cake tin or a 'bundt' tin and fill with ¾ of the above mixture and smoothen out the top. To the rest of the mixture add the cocoa and the remaining sugar and milk. Blend thoroughly. Pile this onto the cake tin over the first mixture. With a fork turn the whole cake mixture gently in a spiral motion all around to get the marble effect. Bake in a moderate oven for approximately 75 minutes. Loosen cake gently with a knife and turn over on to a wire tray to cool. When cool, take out of tin, turn the right way up and sprinkle top with icing sugar.

STRAWBERRY DELIGHT

4 oz. flour	A pinch salt
1 tsp. level baking powder	2 eggs separated
3 oz. castor sugar or, ordinary sugar powdered	1 tsp. vanilla essence
8 heaped tblsp. brandy	

Method

Sieve flour, salt, and baking powder. Mix egg yolk, sugar, and vanilla essence lightly. Add flour mixture to the egg mixture. Mix well. Add egg whites well beaten. Pour into a greased and floured cake tin and bake in med. oven for 20-30 minutes or till done. Alternately microwave at power level "7" (70) for 5-8 minutes. Cool on wire tray and split evenly into 4 rounds. Soak each round with 2 tblsp brandy each before the final assembly.

<u>Filling</u>:

4 litres milk	Juice of 1 small lime or, 1 tblsp. lime juice
4 tblsp. strawberry crush	4 eggs
1 cup cream	

Heat milk. Take off heat and immediately add lime juice stirring continuously till milk curdles. Strain till drained of all water. Mix cheese with beaten eggs and strawberry crush. Put in a dish and microwave for 5 minutes or till set. Alternately, place in the oven and cook till done. Cool and turn out of dish. Beat and mix with cream.

<u>Glaze</u>:

4 tblsp. gelatine	½ cup warm water
2 tsp strawberry crush	

Mix the above in a saucepan and keep stirring over low heat till gelatine dissolves and the mixture begins to thicken. Make the glaze when the dessert is ready just before refrigerating.

Final Assembly:

Sandwich cake layers generously with the above filling. Spread the extra filling on top and sides of the cake to completely cover it. Decorate with whole or split fresh strawberries. Pour glaze over evenly. Refrigerate till required. Serve with fresh cream if desired.

Variations

The eggs for the filling may be omitted. In this case beat the cheese, crush, and cream together well to be able to spread between the cake slices. No need to microwave or put in the oven. Proceed assembling as above.

GERMAN APPLE CAKE

Dough:

2 cups flour sifted	½ cup heaped sugar
2 tsp. baking powder	1 egg
1 tsp. vanilla	6 oz. soft butter

Filling:

4 oz. butter	½ cup sugar
¼ cup flour	4-5 apples peeled, cored, sliced paper thin

Method

Put flour in a ring on a board or table. Put sugar in the centre and flatten. Sprinkle baking powder around on the flour. Lightly beat the egg and mix with the vanilla. Sprinkle this on the sugar. Cut up the butter into small bits and sprinkle all over the flour. Gradually work into the dough with both hands till well mixed and rollable. No need to knead. Grease a spring pan generously. Place dough at the bottom of the pan and spread with the palm to cover the whole and only ½" up the sides. Alternately line a spring pan carefully with grease proof paper without any creases. Oil paper before putting in the dough.

Melt butter in a saucepan. Add sugar and flour and cook till it caramelises and looks like curd. Take off heat and add the apples. Mix well. Put this on the pie shell and bake in a pre-heated moderate oven for about 1 hour. Or till done. Cool on wire tray. Slip out of the frying pan, cut in slices, and serve plain with clotted cream or ordinary fresh cream. Serve as a dessert or with tea or coffee.

CHOCOLATE CAKE

6 oz. butter

2 eggs (3 if small)

2 tsp. baking powder

¼ tsp. salt

1 tsp. vanilla essence

8 oz. sugar

8 oz. flour

¼ tsp. soda

¾ cup milk (may be less0

3 tblsp. cocoa mixed to a paste with 2 tblsp. water

Method

Cream butter and sugar well. Separate eggs. Beat yolks. Add to the butter and sugar mixture and mix. Sift flour, baking powder, soda, and salt. Add little by little the flour mixture alternately with the milk, vanilla and cocoa mixture to the butter and sugar mixture.   Beat egg whites stiff and gradually blend into the cake mixture right at the end. Turn onto a greased and floured cake tin and bake in a moderate oven on the middle shelf for approximately 45 minutes or till done. Test by piercing a cake tester or thin *seekh kabab* stick in the middle of the cake. When ready cool on a wire tray. Serve sprinkled with icing sugar or a simple vanilla or chocolate glaze.

NUT CAKE

350 gm. flour

300 gm. butter

150 gm. nuts ground (any kind – almonds, cashew, peanuts etc.)

1 tsp. baking powder

150 gm. sugar

Method

Sift flour and baking powder together. Beat butter and sugar together till smooth. Add ground nuts of your choice. Mix well. Now fold in the flour mixture and mix with wooden spoon till all well blended. Pour into individual paper cake shells or directly into individual small cake tins. If using paper shells place them in individual small cake tins to hold the shape and preventing the nut cakes from forming unwieldy shapes. Bake in a moderate oven for about 10-15 minutes or till golden. While still hot, roll in a mixture of half icing sugar and half vanillin sugar. (If vanillin sugar is not available flavour fine grained sugar with vanilla essence – do not make it too wet). If using paper cake shells just roll the top in the sugar mixture.

STIR CAKE

3 large eggs or 4 medium eggs	5 tblsp. butter or margarine
1¼ cup sugar	3 tblsp. jam (strawberry, plum, apricot etc.)
1¼ cup flour	2 tsp. baking powder
1 grated lemon rind	5 tblsp. any kind of nut powdered (optional)

Method

Separate eggs. Beat butter, sugar, and yolks together. Add jam 1 tblsp. at a time and keep beating. Sift flour and baking powder together. Powdered nuts and lemon rinds are to be added now. Add to the butter mixture and mix well. Lastly fold in the egg whites beaten stiff. Turn into a greased and floured cake tin and bake in a moderate oven for 45 minutes or till a toothpick inserted in the centre comes out clean. The batter can also be put into individual greased and floured cupcake moulds or in paper cup cake cases which do not need greasing and flouring. Cupcakes take less time to bake. Sprinkle top of big or small cakes with vanillin sugar or plain icing sugar. You can also spread a plain white vanilla glaze or icing on top instead of the dry sugars.

CONGO CAKE

1 kg. sugar

250 gm. butter

2½ tsp. baking powder

¼ tsp. salt

4 tblsp. cocoa powder melted with a little milk or, 4 tblsp. ready coffee, or 2 tblsp. heaped coffee powder.

6 eggs separated

500 gm. flour

8 fluid oz. milk

½ tsp. vanilla essence

2 tblsp. raisins (optional)

Method

Beat sugar, yolks, and butter together. Sift flour and baking powder together and add to the butter mixture little by little alternating with the milk. Beat egg whites stiff with salt and vanilla essence. Gradually fold into the flour and butter mixture. Divide the cake dough and spread half onto a rectangular buttered but not floured baking tray or cake tin smoothly. Add the cocoa or coffee to the rest of the cake dough and mix well. Spread this over the white dough and smoothen the top. Sprinkle raisins on top. Bake in a moderate oven for 40 minutes or till one. Sprinkle powdered sugar on top before serving.

FEATHER-WEIGHT SPONGE

(This is ideally suited for a sponge-based dessert or, just a plain tea-time gateau.)

   4 oz. castor sugar   3 eggs

   3 oz. sifted flour

Method

Cover heat-resistant plate with foil. Spread the sugar evenly on this and put it on the middle shelf of a pre- heated moderately hot oven. Keep for approximately 5 minutes.

Line a Swiss roll tin (14" × 10" × ¾") with grease proof paper. Oil the paper and the sides of the tin. Break eggs in a bowl one at a time and beat together lightly. Tip the piping hot sugar onto the eggs and whisk vigorously till a pale golden foam rising well up the sides of the bowl. Add sifted flour to the mixture and gently blend with a spatula without beating. Spread evenly onto the paper lined Swiss roll tin right up to the corners. This part is very important or else the sponge will be very uneven when ready and difficult to roll. Bake for 8-10 minutes in a pre-heated moderately hot oven till golden. When pressed it should feel like a sponge. Turn onto a sugared grease-proof paper or cheese cloth. Quickly roll tightly holding onto the edges of the paper/cloth. Unroll, spread with filling of your choice and re-roll. Sprinkle with castor or icing sugar.

Alternatively, the sponge may be baked in a spring or ordinary oven proof round oiled and floured bowl. When ready the sponge should feel like a spring when pressed. Turn onto a wire tray to cool. Sandwich with any filling of your choice. This sponge can be used for any of your favourite dessert or cake recipes which require the basic sponge.

SPONGE GATEAU

Sponge:

7-8-9 eggs	12 tblsp. level sugar
7-8-9 tblsp. heaped (depending on the number of eggs used) flour	2-3 tsp. baking soda

Method

Separate eggs. Beat whites stiff. Add sugar 1 tblsp at a time beating continuously. Add the yolks a little at a time and continue beating after each addition. Add the flour, which has been sifted with the baking powder, gradually a little at a time and continue mixing till all well blended. Bake in a greased, floured round or square cake tin in a hot oven for approx. 30 minutes.

Filling:

8-10 oz. fresh heavy/double cream	5 tblsp. cocoa or substitute or, instant coffee or any jam (if using jam, reduce the quantity of sugar)
10-11 tblsp. crystal sugar	

Beat all the above ingredients together till well blended.

Assembly:

Cut cake into three layers. Sandwich the layers with the filling. If any extra filling is left over, spread the top and sides of the cake with it. Refrigerate till required. Can decorate the top with cherries, walnuts, or almonds.

Variations: Cashew Nut Cake – Make a sponge as above but substitute powdered cashew nuts instead of flour. Sandwich with the above filling substituting finely chopped cashew nut instead of cocoa.

MOCHA CAKE

8 eggs separated	10 oz. sugar
6 oz. sifted potato flour or, ½ flour and ½ corn flour	½ lemon (approx. 1 tsp.) juice

Method

Beat egg yolks and sugar till pale and frothy. Fold in stiffly beaten egg whites along with the flour and lemon juice. Put mixture in a buttered cake tin in a very slow oven (275^0F) for about 1 hour or till done. Cool on wire tray. Remove from tin and cut in 3-4 layers. Sandwich with mocha cream. Dust top with powdered, castor or icing sugar. Alternately spread some of the butter cream on top and sides and decorate with toasted walnut crumbs.

Mocha Butter Cream:

4 egg yolks	4 oz. sugar
10 oz. soft unsalted butter	4 tblsp. triple strength coffee

Method

Beat egg yolks with sugar and when light and frothy add the butter and beat for at least 30 minutes. An electric beater is more convenient. While still beating add the coffee rapidly.

Alternately make a thick custard with sugar, egg and 1 litre milk. be sure not to let the custard curdle or form lumps. Cook on low heat stirring constantly with a wooden spoon. When cool proceed as above.

VIENNA ROLLS

50gm. or, 5 tsp. yeast

1 tblsp. sugar

1-1¼ cup cold milk

1 cup butter

4-5 cups flour

Extra butter and sugar

Method

Mix yeast with a little sugar and a little lukewarm milk or, according to the directions on the package. Stir butter and sugar together. Add flour, yeast, and milk. Stir to mix well. It should be rolling consistency. If too dry add a little milk. If too liquid add a little flour. Roll out on a floured board ¼" thick. Cut in small squares. Put 1 tsp. butter and ½ tsp. sugar in the centre of each square. Draw the sides carefully to fold over and cover the butter and sugar. Lay each square on cupcake paper cases. Arrange on a baking tray. Keep in room temperature for about 3 hours. to rise. Brush with egg yolk. Bake in a hot oven for 5-7 minutes. These rolls should be eaten on the day of baking. They do not keep too long and tend to harden.

TANGY SPONGE CAKE

6 eggs

14 oz. sugar

1 tsp. heaped baking powder

4 tblsp. fresh orange or, lemon juice

10 oz. flour

Method

Proceed mixing the above ingredients as the sponge gateau. Bake in a moderate oven for approximately 20 minutes or till done. Serve sprinkled with castor/icing/powdered sugar on top.

Note

Bottled or canned orange /lemon juice may be substituted. In this case reduce the amount of sugar to 10-12 oz. depending on the sweetness of the juice. 1 tsp grated lemon or orange rind may be added with the dry ingredients if desired.

SPONGE FOR TORTES

4 eggs separated	3-4 tblsp. lukewarm water
150 gm. sugar	1 tsp. vanilla essence
100 gm. flour	100 gm. corn starch or, corn flour
3 tsp. level baking powder	

Method

Beat egg yolks with water till creamy. Add the sugar and vanilla gradually. Beat egg whites stiff and put on top of the above mixture. Mix flour, corn flour and baking powder and then sieve all on top of the egg whites. Mix slowly and carefully. Bake in a pre-heated moderate oven till done – about 10-15 minutes or a little more.

Prepare sponge a day before. Cut in 2-3 layers and sandwich with any of the following fillings. Sprinkle top of cake with castor sugar.

Orange Filling:

25 gm. corn starch or corn flour	150 gm. sugar
250 gm. butter	4 liquid oz. fresh or concentrated orange juice
3/8 litre water	3/8 litre water

Mix all the above ingredients and cook on low heat in a double boiler or over a pan of water till thick and spreadable. Cool and spread between layers of sponge.

Lemon Filling:

Cook 1 pkt. of lemon flavoured blancmange pudding according to instructions. Cool and spread as above.

Chocolate Filling:

Cook 1 packet chocolate flavoured pudding according to instructions and spread as above.

Alternately, follow the recipe for the orange filling. Omit the orange juice and add 1-2 tblsp cocoa powder. Increase the sugar according to taste.

A third variation of the chocolate filling would be to melt 2 bars of good milk chocolate in a double boiler. This must be spread quickly or the chocolate will set, in which case return it on low heat till it begins to melt once again.

PLAIN SPONGE CAKE

5 large eggs

6 oz. castor sugar

6 oz. flour

1 tsp. baking powder

1 tsp. orange or lemon rind grated

Method

Separate the eggs. Beat the egg whites stiff. Add the sugar gradually a little at a time continuing to beat after each addition. Next add the yolks a little at a time beating after each addition. Sift flour and baking powder together. Add the rind and mix gently. Fold the dry ingredients into the egg mixture and stir till all well blended. Pour mixture into a greased and floured cake pan and bake in a medium oven for ½ hour to 45 minutes. Turn out on a wire tray and cool. Split cake into three layers and sandwich with any of the following fillings. Sprinkle top of cake with castor or icing sugar.

Orange or Lemon Filling:

4 tblsp. unsalted butter

2 tblsp. corn flour

2 tblsp. lemon juice or 2 tblsp. grated lemon rind

<u>OR</u> 4 tblsp. orange juice or 1 tblsp. grated orange rind

1-2 eggs

Combine all the above ingredients in a saucepan and cook in a double boiler or over a larger pan of warm water, stirring continuously with a wooden spoon until mixture thickens and is the consistency of jam. Cool and sandwich in between the cake layers.

Chocolate Filling:

Use the same ingredients and method as above except substitute 2 tblsp cocoa omitting the orange and lemon juices and rinds.

Coffee Filling:

Prepare as the chocolate filling substituting 2 tsp instant coffee powder or 2 tblsp strong brewed coffee.

Mocha Filling:

Prepare as the chocolate filling adding 2 tsp coffee powder or 2 tblsp strong brewed coffee.

Cream Cheese Filling:

1254 gm. cream cheese	1 or 2 eggs
4 tblsp. castor sugar	1-2 tblsp. corn flour

Mix all the above ingredients in a saucepan flavouring with any of the following: vanilla, sherry, rum, finely chopped fresh strawberries/pineapple or strawberry/pineapple essence, orange, or lemon juice or any other flavouring preferred. Cook as in all the above fillings.

PARTY CUP CAKES

4 oz. butter/margarine

4 oz. castor sugar

2 large eggs

6 oz. flour

1 tsp. level baking powder

A pinch salt

2-4 tblsp (more or less) milk/water

Method

Beat butter and sugar until creamy. Whisk eggs and add to the butter mixture beating continuously. Sift dry ingredients and gently stir into the mixture. Add enough milk to get a dropping consistency. Grease and flour cupcake moulds. Half fill with batter. Bake in a moderate oven till done. Alternately place paper cup cake cases in the cupcake moulds and half fill with batter. This way there will be less washing up to do and each cake will be in its own case. Decorate with a glacé icing or minced cherries which should be sprinkled during the last few mins of baking. Can sprinkle with icing or castor sugar when done.

Variations

The cupcakes can be varied by adding any of the following combinations.

1. Chocolate: Add 1 oz cocoa or grated bakers' chocolate to the dry ingredients. Add 1 tsp vanilla essence at the end. Decorate the cakes with chocolate glacé icing.

2. Coconut: Add 1 oz desiccated coconut to the dry ingredients, ½ tsp vanilla essence and a few drops of pink colouring (optional) with the milk.

3. Lemon OR Orange: Add 1 tblsp (or less) grated lemon/orange rind to the dry ingredients. Decorate with lemon/orange glacé icing.

4. Butterfly Orange/Lemon/Coconut Cakes: Cut a thin slice from top of cakes. Halve each slice to resemble two wings. Dredge the wings with icing sugar. Spread the cut tops of cakes with any jam. Pipe a rosette of thick double cream or place a dollop of cream on the jam. Stick the cake slices into the cream to look like wings. Instead of cream a thick dollop of custard made with corn flour instead of custard powder could be substituted. This is a great hit at kiddie parties!

MADELEINES

Basic Sponge:

4 oz. butter or margarine	4 oz. castor sugar
2 eggs well beaten	4 oz. flour sieved
2 tsp. (approx.) cold milk	1 bottle strawberry jam
1 cup (more or less) desiccated coconut	8 cherries halved

Angelica for garnish (optional)

12 *madeleine* moulds – these are cone shaped with a little flat bottom. Approximate measurements – 1" at the bottom, 2" on top and height.

Method

Beat butter and sugar till creamy. Add the beaten eggs and mix well. Now add the flour a little at a time till all well mixed. Add enough milk to make the dough a little moist. Grease 12 madeleine moulds with butter making sure the bottoms of the tins are well greased. Fill the moulds ¾ way up with the dough. Place the tins on a flat baking tray for convenience. Bake in a moderately hot oven in the middle shelf for about 15-20 minutes. Test for doneness by inserting a tooth- pick in the centre. If it comes out clean the cakes are done. Take the cakes out of the mould while still hot by inverting them on a wire tray and tapping the bottom (narrow part) gently. In the meantime, take the jam out of the bottle and pour into a saucepan. Heat till it becomes a little liquid. Spread the coconut on a plate. When the cakes are cool, carefully dip them one at a time in the jam and then roll in the desiccated coconut. Decorate tops with a half cherry or cherry and angelica. Once the madeleines are out of their moulds they should look almost like pyramids.

If madeleine moulds are not available, make these cakes in small cake moulds or in a round or square cake tin. Of course, the effect will not be the same.

If using fresh grated coconut, make sure it is dry. This can be done in the oven or in the sun making sure it does not brown. It should be white like snow.

SEMLOR (SWEDISH CAKE)

1¼ cup milk

25 gm. dry yeast

200-250 gm. flour

5 almonds chopped fine

50 gm. butter melted

½-1 cup sugar

1-1½ cardamom powdered

Method

Mix milk with the melted butter. Heat to just lukewarm. Mix the dry yeast with the sugar and only 1/3 of the flour. Add to it the lukewarm milk and butter mixture. Stir for 2 minutes. Add the cardamom, almonds, and sufficient flour to make a thin dough. Keep covered in a warm place to rise. Knead on a floured board well for about 20-25 minutes. Alternately knead in a kitchen machine or food processor. Roll into small balls and arrange on a greased baking tray. Place tray over boiling water till double in size. Bake in a hot oven for about 5-8 minutes. When ready, take out and brush tops with cold water. Let cool and then split each cake in half. Sandwich with the following filling, sprinkle top with icing sugar and serve with tea or coffee.

Filling:

40 gm. almonds blanched and powdered

1 egg white

¼-½ cup whipped cream

40 gm. icing sugar

1 tsp. lime juice

Combine all the above ingredients except the cream. Sandwich each cake with the filling topped with some cream.

Variation

These cakes may also be served as dessert with a syrup of sufficient milk, sugar, and cinnamon powder to taste all boiled together.

CREAM CAKE (I)

This is basically made with the top of the milk. It is the cream collected from the top of the milk after boiling and the scrapings from the bottom and sides of the pan. And yes, it does need long time planning. The cream is collected till the required amount is reached. this must be kept in the freezer till used. This can be served as dessert or cut in slices as a cake.

2 cups top of the milk	1 cup or more sugar
4 eggs	1 tsp. vanilla/strawberry or any other essence or flavouring
4 oz. flour	1 tsp. baking powder

Method

Beat the top of milk with the sugar till well blended. Add eggs one by one and keep beating till thoroughly mixed. Add the essence. Sift flour and baking powder together and then gradually add to the mixture mixing gently with a wooden spoon or with an electric hand beater. Turn into a cake pan (greased and floured) and bake in a moderate oven for ½ hour – 45 minutes or, till done.

If served as a dessert fresh cream may be served with it. Alternately honey or any other syrup such as strawberry/ raspberry /lemon/orange etc. may also be served with it.

Variation

Paneer or Cottage Cheesecake: Proceed as the Cream Cake above replacing top of milk with cottage cheese.

CREAM CAKE (II)

8 oz, cream (top of milk)

2-4 tblsp. castor sugar

2-3 eggs

1 tsp. vanilla essence (optional)

Method

Mix all the above ingredients and beat thoroughly till smooth. Place in a well-greased and floured or non-stick cake pan and bake in a very low oven till set. Serve, cut in slices or with cream.

Variations

Add 1-2 tblsp of raisins just before pouring mixture into the cake pan. Thick cream or "*khoa*" – milk boiled down to a quarter of the original quantity can be used if a sufficient amount of top of milk is not available.

CARROT CAKE

8 oz. sugar

8 oz. flour

1 tsp. baking powder

A pinch of salt

¼ tsp. ginger powder

¼ tsp. clove powder

4 oz. oil

2 eggs

4 oz. sour cream or, yogurt

12 oz. carrot finely grated

Method

Sift all the dry ingredients together. Make a well in the centre and pour in the oil. Mix with a wooden spoon by gradually drawing the flour from the sides. Next add the eggs one at a time mixing the dough gently after each addition. When the mixture is well blended add the sour cream slowly, stirring continuously. Last of all mix the grated carrot making sure all the ingredients are well incorporated. Bake in a greased and floured 9" × 2" round or an 8" × 8" square cake tin, or a 1lb. loaf tin in a moderate oven for approximately 45 minutes (more or less), depending on individual ovens.

Variation

Pumpkin Cake: Substitute red pumpkin in place of carrot and proceed as the Carrot Cake. (Both pumpkin and carrot may be grated or cooked and mashed before adding to the cake mixture). Also, substitute ¼ to ½ tsp. mixed spice in place of clove powder. ¼ tsp. cinnamon powder may also be used.

WINTER SPONGE CAKE

8 oz. butter	8 oz. sugar
4 eggs	2 large juicy oranges – extract the juice
2 tblsp. rum	1 tblsp. orange rind (fresh or dried) grated
A pinch of salt	2 tsp. rounded baking powder
8 oz. flour	

Method

Beat butter and sugar till creamy consistency. Add the eggs one at a time. Keep beating after each addition till well mixed. Mix the orange juice and rum and add to the cream mixture along with the rind. Beat all together so that it is well mixed. Now sieve all the dry ingredients together. Make a well in the centre and pour the cream mixture into it. Gradually draw the flour mixture from all sides into the well and mix gently with a wooden spoon. Keep stirring and mixing till well blended and there are no lumps. The mixture should be smooth. Grease and flour a 9" cake spring pan. Pour the batter in and even out with a wooden spoon. Make sure the centre is not too high. Better to smoothen the sides on top and make a depression in the centre with the back of the spoon. This way the cake will rise evenly instead of like a mountain in the centre. Bake in a moderately hot oven for about 1 hour. When ready turn over on a wire tray to cool. This cake keeps for a long time in a cool place preferably in the refrigerator. Icing sugar could be sprinkled on top before serving or a thin glaze poured over it. On the other hand, it could be served plain.

EASY CHRISTMAS CAKE

For this cake follow the method for Winter Orange Cake leaving out the orange juice, and rum. Instead use:

2 tblsp. raisins	1-2 tblsp. sultanas
3 tsp. or more brandy	3 tsp. heaped soft *jaggery*

Any other preserves may be added or substituted e.g. cherries cut small, currants etc. A few cherries could be kept aside for decoration on top.

Method

Soak the raisins, sultanas, orange rind (preferably dried or crystallized) and any other preserves if used, in the brandy overnight or for several hours. Proceed as Winter Orange Cake blending in the *jaggery* evenly with the creamy mixture. Stir the soaked preserves with the liquid, if any, into the cake batter at the last minute just before pouring it into the cake tin. This cake can also be served plain or with a sprinkling of icing sugar on top or with a thin glaze all around. The cake will keep for a long time just like the Winter Orange Cake.

ICEBOX CHRISTMAS CAKE

4 oz. raisins or, 2 oz. raisins & 2 oz. dates

2 oz. sultanas

8 oz. marshmallows cut in small pieces

4 oz. pecan nuts/walnuts/almonds/peanuts

12-13 oz. (approx.) condensed milk

2 oranges – rinds only grated

2-4 cups ordinary sweet biscuits broken

2 oz. currants

3 oz. desiccated coconut

4-5 glacé cherries

1½ tblsp. brandy/rum

A pinch of salt

3 oz. candied peels chopped

Method

Chop all the above ingredients fine and then mix all together well. Line a loaf or cake tin (or any other container) with wax paper. Put the cake mixture in and press and pack in as much as possible. Cover top completely with more wax paper. Take out of container carefully without spoiling the shape and secure well all round with any mode of tie e.g. string/rubber band etc. Place in a polythene bag, securing opening tightly with another tie or place in a zip lock back. Refrigerate for a minimum of 1 week before cutting and serving in slices. This cake keeps for a long time. After cutting the few slices required it should be re-wrapped and put back in the refrigerator. Do not freeze. This cake can be served plain or with cream, clotted cream, sweetened cream, or cottage cheese. It can also be flambéed. However, it is delicious just served plain.

CHOCOLATE ICEBOX CAKE

1-2 lbs. sponge cake slices or, boudoir (sponge biscuits)

3 oz. Fine sugar

¼ pt. milk

4 oz. chocolate – any kind

4 egg yolks

¼ cup sherry, brandy, or rum

6-8 cherries (optional)

Topping:

1 cup double cream or unsalted butter

2-3 lbs, grated chocolate or, chocolate nibs

1-2 tblsp. castor or icing sugar – (optional)

Method

Line the bottom and sides of a round or square cake pan or any baking dish with grease proof or waxed paper or aluminium foil leaving about an inch over the top. Arrange the sponge slices around the sides and bottom of the dish. Heat water in a saucepan. Lower heat to medium and beat the yolks and sugar in another bowl over the hot water till smooth and creamy. This can be also done in a double boiler. Melt the chocolate in the milk and add to egg mixture. Now add the sherry or substitute. Whisk all together till well blended. Sprinkle some cherries cut in half over the cake and then pour the chocolate mixture over it till it reaches the top. Add more sponge slices and the remaining chocolate mixture. Cover with foil and leave in the refrigerator for about 12 hours. Turn out on a serving dish decorate with cream or butter beaten with icing sugar. Lightly sprinkle grated chocolate or chocolate nibs. Refrigerate till required. Cut in slices and serve.

SPICED WHEAT CAKE

8 oz. castor sugar

4 eggs

2 tsp. heaped baking powder

½ tsp. nutmeg

½ tsp. cinnamon powder

10 oz. butter or margarine

8 oz. brown wheat flour

½ tsp. mace

½ tsp. ginger powder

½ tsp. allspice

Method

Bear sugar and butter till smooth. Add the eggs one at a time and continue beating till well blended. Sift all the dry ingredients together and fold into the butter mixture till all well mixed with no lumps in the batter. Pour into a greased and floured cake pan and bake in a medium hot oven for about 1-1½ hours. Sprinkle top with icing or castor sugar or spread top of cake with a standard vanilla, lemon, orange, rum, or brandy butter icing. This is a delicious cake with or without the icing.

DELICIOUS WHOLE WHEAT SPICE CAKE

6 oz. any *vanaspati* (hydrogenated oil) or 8 oz. butter/margarine

8 oz. brown sugar

3 tsp. baking powder

4 eggs

½ tsp. ginger powder

¼ tsp. nutmeg powder

A pinch of salt

¼ tsp. mace powder

8 oz. whole wheat sifted

Method

Beat the fat with the sugar. Add the eggs one by one and continue beating till light and smooth. Mix all the dry ingredients together and then add to the egg mixture. Mix well making sure the mixture is well blended and there are no lumps. Pour into a greased and floured 9" round cake pan and bake in a moderate oven for about 1 hour or till a fork inserted into the centre of the cake comes out clean. Loosen cake from the tin and turn over onto a wire tray to cool. Slice and serve with tea/coffee or as a dessert with cream.

CHOCOLATE WHEAT CAKE

6 oz. butter

2 eggs

2 tsp. baking powder

8 oz. powdered or castor sugar

8 oz. wheat flour

2 tsp. cocoa

Method

Beat butter and sugar till light and fluffy. Add the eggs one at a time beating well after each addition. Sift the dry ingredients together and gradually add to the butter mixture beating after each addition to blend well. Pour into a greased and floured cake pan and bake in a moderately hot oven for about 45 minutes to 1hour. When cool, sprinkle top with castor or icing sugar or ice top of cake with chocolate butter icing. Alternately this cake can be served in slices as a dessert topped with ice cream or accompanied with custard or cream. The cake can also be flambéed with brandy and served in slices with ice cream, custard, or cream.

CHOCOLATE SPONGE CAKE

2 eggs	4 oz. fresh milk
1 tsp. vanilla essence	6 oz. unsalted butter softened
6 oz. castor or, powdered sugar	8 oz. flour
½ tsp. bicarbonate of soda or, baking powder	4 tblsp. heaped cocoa powder

Method

Beat the eggs and milk and vanilla together and keep aside. In another bowl beat the butter and sugar till fluffy and add to the egg mixture. Blend well. Sift the flour, soda bicarb and cocoa together and gradually fold into the above mixture stirring continuously till all well blended. Turn into a greased and floured oven proof dish and bake in a medium hot oven for about ½ hr to 45 mins. Turn onto a wire tray and let cake cool. Coat top and sides with the following chocolate icing.

Chocolate Icing:

1 tblsp. unsalted butter	1 cup (or more) icing sugar
2-4 tblsp. cocoa	Hot water as required

Melt butter in a saucepan over hot water or in a double boiler. Add the sugar and cocoa together and keep stirring. The amount of cocoa depends on how dark a cake is required. Add the hot water only if necessary. Be careful not to make the icing too runny or too stiff. It should reach a spreading consistency. Cool and spread over and around cake.

Variation

a. Make some extra icing – approximately double the above quantity. Cut cake into 2 layers and sandwich with the icing

b. Melt 1 or 2 slabs of sweet chocolate in a double boiler or in a saucepan over hot water. Use this to sandwich the cake. Melted chocolate can also be used to ice the cake on top and sides instead of the icing given above.

CHOCOLATE ALMOND CAKE

4 oz. unsalted butter softened

8 oz. sugar

3 eggs separated

1 tsp. almond essence

1 lb. flour

1 tsp. soda-bicarbonate or baking powder

2-4 tblsp. milk

Method

Beat butter and sugar till fluffy. Add the yolks one at a time and keep beating continuously to mix well. Add the almond essence and stir well. Sift flour and baking powder and then gradually fold into the cake mixture stirring to mix well. Beat the egg whites stiff and gently fold into the mixture. At this time add just enough milk to get a moist consistency. It should not be too soft and sticky. Bake in a greased and floured cake tin in a moderately hot oven for about 45 minutes. Turn onto a wire tray to cool. Ice top and sides of cake with chocolate icing as in chocolate sponge cake or with melted sweet chocolate. Decorate by completely or partially covering with thin slices of almond. Leave in the refrigerator for several hours or overnight before slicing into serving pieces.

Variation

While making the cake add 3 tblsp cocoa to the dry ingredients before sifting. Increase the almond essence by ½ tsp. Continue the rest of the procedure as given above.

PATALI (DATE JAGGERY) CAKE

("*Patali Gur*" is a specialty and favourite of Bengal. It is normally available during the winter months but now-a-days it seems to be available almost throughout the year. It has a very special flavour unlike other jaggeries and is eaten plain with any Indian bread especially "*puris*". It also lends flavour to the Bengali '*payesh*', – a dessert of thickened full cream milk and rice minus the sugar. The required quantity of grated *patali* is added, for sweetness and flavour at the end, after the dessert has cooled or else the milk will curdle.)

4-6 oz. *patali gur* grated	6 oz. any shortening
2 tblsp brown sugar	4 eggs
1 tsp banana essence (optional)	8 oz flour
2 tsp baking powder	1 tsp ginger powder

Method

Beat the *patali*, shortening and sugar well till creamy, light, and fluffy. This can be done in the food processor. Add the eggs one at a time beating after each addition. Add the banana essence and stir to mix. Sift the flour, baking powder and ginger powder together and then add to the *patali* mixture. Blend well. Pour into a greased and floured cake tin and bake in a moderate oven for 45 minutes to 1 hour or, till done. Cool on a wire tray. Slice and serve with tea or coffee or as a dessert with fresh cream or plain vanilla ginger ice cream.

COCK-EYED EGGLESS CHOCOLATE CAKE

3 cups flour

2 tsp. level soda

1 tsp. salt

2 tblsp. red vinegar

2 cups cold water

6 tblsp. cocoa

2 cups sugar

10 tblsp. oil

2 tsp. vanilla essence

9" × 9" × 2" baking dish

Method

Grease bottom and sides of baking dish well (which, if necessary, may also be used as a serving dish at the table). Sift the flour, cocoa, soda, sugar, and salt in the dish. Spread gently and make three holes in the dry mixture. Divide and pour oil, vinegar, and vanilla into each of the holes. Pour the water over the whole mixture. Beat mixture with a wooden spoon in the dish till the texture is smooth. Place baking dish in a moderate oven and bake for ½ hour or till done. This cake can be served cut in slices with tea or coffee or as a dessert accompanied with a chocolate syrup and fresh cream.

Variation

If preferred, sift the dry ingredients together in a separate bowl and then add the oil, vinegar and vanilla and mix well. Last of all add the water and beat manually with a wooden spoon or with an electric hand beater till smooth. Pour mixture into a greased cake pan and bake as above. After cooling the cake, it can be split in the middle once or twice and sandwiched with chocolate cream and also spread on top. However, the original method of mixing the ingredients has a better result.

PASTRY ALMOND CAKE

Pastry:

4 oz. flour	2 tsp. sugar powdered
3 oz. butter	2-4 tblsp. (more or less) ice-water

Method

Mix flour and sugar. Rub butter into the flour mixture very quickly till resembles breadcrumbs. Now add ice-water very little at a time to form a soft, pliable dough. The dough should not be too sticky or too dry. Use two knives or wooden spoons to form the dough as long as possible. Only, if necessary, use the fingers at the last minute to form into a ball. Be very quick in making this dough. Cover with a cloth or small bowl and leave in the refrigerator till required.

Cake:

2 oz. butter	4 oz. sugar
2 eggs	½ tsp. almond essence
4 oz. flour	2 tsp. baking powder
A pinch of salt	4 almonds ground

Beat butter and sugar till light and fluffy. Add the eggs one at a time beating continuously. Add the almond essence and stir to mix. Sift the rest of the dry ingredients except almonds and mix with the butter mixture.

Brush a cake pan with butter. Sprinkle lightly with breadcrumbs. Take out pastry from the refrigerator and place on a floured board. Pat with a rolling pin and roll to fit the base of the cake pan. Line cake pan with the pastry making sure all the sides are even. Pour the cake mixture over the pastry and spread gently and evenly. Sprinkle the ground almond on top. Bake in a pre-heated moderate oven for ½ hour–45 minutes or until a skewer pierced in the middle of the cake comes out clean.

Variation: Any other flavouring can be substituted for almond e.g. orange, lemon, chocolate, coffee etc. Omit the ground almond and use orange/lemon rind, chocolate chips/nibs/grated or walnuts/peanuts for coffee flavouring as the case maybe.

BESTING CAKE (GERMAN)

Batter:

250 gm. flour	1-2 tsp. level baking powder
150 gm. butter	100 gm. sugar
4 eggs	A little milk if required

Filling:

75 gm. butter	100 gm. sugar
1 packet (1-2 tblsp.) vanilla sugar	1 tblsp. milk or, cream
150 gm. almonds peeled and ground	

Method

For the batter – Sift the flour and baking powder and keep aside. Beat the butter and sugar till creamy. Beat in the eggs gradually one by one. When mixture is creamy, fold in the flour and stir gently to mix. If too dry, add a little milk. Pour into a greased baking cake tin and spread the top evenly. Cover with the filling and bake in a moderately hot oven for 35–40 minutes till golden brown.

For the Filling – Mix all the ingredients except the almonds in a pan and stir over low heat. When the butter has melted, and all the ingredients are well blended, take off heat and stir in the almonds. Cool before spreading on the above batter.

PLAIN CAKE WITH OIL

4 eggs separated

¾ cup sugar (castor or powdered)

½-¾ cup any white oil

1 tsp. vanilla essence

1 cup flour

1 tsp. baking powder

Method

Beat the egg yolks with the sugar. Add the oil gradually and keep beating. Now add the vanilla. This can be done in the food processor, blender or with an electric hand beater. Sift the flour and baking powder and add to the egg mixture. Beat the egg whites stiff and then fold into the cake mixture. Pour into a buttered and floured cake tin. Bake in a moderate oven for 45minutes– 1 hour.

SOUTHEAST ASIAN CASAVA COCONUT CAKE

2 eggs

3 tblsp. butter/margarine melted

1 cup fresh cassava grated

4 tblsp. any un-flavoured cheese grated

¾ cup sugar

¾ cup coconut cream/milk*

½ cup coconut jelly (from a tender green coconut) sliced

* Coconut cream/milk is now available in cans everywhere which is recommended for this recipe rather than fresh coconut milk

Method

Beat eggs. Add sugar, butter, and coconut cream. Blend well. Add the cassava and coconut jelly. Stir to mix well. Next add the cheese and again mix well. Line a baking tray with banana leaves or wax paper and pour the mixture into it. Spread with the back of a spoon or knife to even and smoothen out the top as is done when baking a cake. Bake in a moderate oven till done. Test with a toothpick inserted in the centre of the cake which should come out clean. Cut in slices and serve with cream if desired.

Variations

Sweet potatoes can be substituted in place of cassava. The baking tray may also be lined with foil.

COOKIES

TASTY COOKIES

12½ tblsp. margarine or butter

2 tsp. vanilla essence

500 gm. flour

5 tblsp. ground almonds or, cashew nuts, or powdered chocolate or, powdered cinnamon

5 tblsp. heaped castor sugar

1 egg

3 tsp. baking powder

Method

Mix all the above. Shape with the biscuit cutter of a kitchen machine or, roll out ¼" thick and cut with a cookie cutter or just shape by hand. Decorate with crystallized fruit or nuts. Place in greased and floured baking sheets. Bake in a hot oven 5-10 minutes.

Variation:

Salty cookies:

Use 5 tblsp cottage cheese or any other flavoured or plain cooking cheese grated. Omit sugar and vanilla essence. Add salt according to taste, (some cheeses may be saltier than others). 2 tsp of caraway or whole cumin seeds may be used as flavouring. Can also use 1 tsp paprika to give the savoury cookies the extra zip. Omit the fruits or nuts for the decoration and use whole cumin or caraway seeds instead.

CSOROGE* (HUNGARIAN)

*Pronounced "Choroge"

2 tblsp. fresh cream

2 eggs

1 cup oil

1 tblsp. castor sugar

10 tblsp. flour sifted

For Sprinkling:

Vanillin sugar or, icing sugar or, cinnamon powder or, a mixture of the two latter items.

Method

Mix fresh cream and sugar till well blended. Add eggs one at a time and blend after each addition. Now add the sifted flour a little at a time and continue to mix with a wooden spoon. Roll out thin on a floured board. Cut with a sharp knife into narrow, long rectangular shapes or like cheese straws. Make a small slit all the way in the centre of each shape. Now heat oil in a small wok and deep fry the csoroges in batches. Drain on paper towels. When all done roll them in any of the above or a combination of the sugars and spices of your choice.

QUICK-MIX CHOCOLATE COOKIES

30 oz. flour

5 tblsp. castor sugar

2 large eggs

3 tblsp. cocoa

7 oz. margarine

Method

Sift flour and cocoa together. Add the castor sugar and mix well. Next add the softened margarine and mix till like breadcrumbs. Now add the eggs one at a time slightly beaten. Mix all well. If your kitchen mix or food processor has a cookie cutter attachment, then put the mixture through it and place on a greased and floured baking tray. If you need to roll out the dough and cut the cookies manually then, you may need an extra egg or two and another 2-3 oz. additional margarine to bind the dough. Do not use too much margarine or the dough will crumble and become unmanageable when in the oven. Roll out the dough to a ¼" thickness before cutting. Bake the cookies for 15-20 minutes in a moderate oven.

Variations

For plain vanilla cookies omit the cocoa and add 1 tsp vanilla essence with the addition of the last egg. Similarly strawberry, lemon, orange, raspberry etc essences may be substituted. Instead of using orange essence, 2-4 tblsp fresh or 1-2 concentrated orange juice may be added.

CHOCOLATE COOKIES

½ cup. Butter or margarine

1 cup sugar

2 squares unsweetened chocolate, melted or, 1 cup cocoa powder

1 egg

¾ cup butter milk

½ tsp. salt

1¾ cup flour

½ tsp. baking soda

1 cup nuts chopped fine – hazel, walnuts, or almonds

1 tsp. vanilla essence

Method

In a bowl mix butter, sugar, melted and cooled chocolate (if using cocoa powder make into a paste with very little water) and egg thoroughly. Stir in buttermilk and vanilla. In another bowl sift flour, salt, and soda. Blend in the nuts. Add this to the first mixture. Spread in a greased and lightly floured square tray. Chill in the refrigerator for about 1 hour. Bake in a hot oven for 8-10 minutes. Turn out from tray when ready. While still warm (not hot or cool) cut into cookies. Frost with a thin white icing.

CHOCOLATE VANILLA COOKIES

11 oz. castor sugar

1 tsp. vanilla essence

1-2 tblsp. milk

8 oz. butter

1 lb. flour sifted

2 tblsp. cocoa

Method

Beat the 8 oz. sugar and butter and vanilla till well blended. Add the flour gradually and mix well. Add enough milk only if necessary to bind the dough. Divide the dough in two halves. To one half of the dough add the cocoa and 3 oz sugar and mix till no white shows. Now roll out both the halves separately into a little less than ¼" thickness. Cut in rounds of 1" diameter. Now take a chocolate round and place on a vanilla round. Gently press down and seal the edges carefully with fingers. After joining the halves, the rounds should not be more than ¼" in thickness. They should not be too thin or else they will become too 'wafery'. Also, the edges should be well sealed, or they will separate during baking. Lay the cookies on a greased and floured baking tray and bake in a moderate oven for 15 minutes or till ready. Just before the cookies are ready sprinkle a little granulated sugar on top of each. Alternately sprinkle icing sugar on top before serving or glace the cookies. Store in a container with a tight-fitting lid.

UNCOOKED CHOCOLATE BISCUITS

4 oz. butter

4 oz. castor sugar

1 large egg or substitute*, or 1-2 tblsp. cream, or top of milk

3 tblsp. cocoa

2 oz. washed and deseeded sultanas

2 oz. chopped walnuts

8 oz. plain sweet biscuits

Topping:

3-8 oz. sweet chocolate melted over hot water

¼ pt. double cream (optional)

* Please see "Miscellaneous" section of this book.

Method

Melt butter in a pan. Add sugar, stir, and allow to cool slightly. Beat eggs tightly and stir into the mixture with the cocoa. Crush biscuits finely with a rolling pin or in the food processor. Add to the mixture with the sultanas and walnuts. Spread mixture in a greased Swiss roll tin and press down hard. Cover with '*Clingwrap*' or foil and let stand in the refrigerator overnight. Next day take out of the refrigerator, uncover, and spread with the Topping. Let set and then cut in squares or triangles or any other shape

----

SIMPLE HOME-BAKED COOKIES

2 lbs. flour

7 oz. margarine

2 tsp. baking powder

2-4 tblsp. milk for mixing

1 tblsp. chopped nuts -- any kind (optional)

12 oz. icing sugar

2 eggs

1 tsp. vanilla essence (can substitute rum, sherry, or brandy)

Method

Mix all the above ingredients except nuts, using only 1 egg. Use enough milk to get a soft consistency – should not be too dry or too sticky. Roll out to ¼" thickness and cut into any shape. Place on a greased and floured cookie sheet. Brush tops with the remaining egg. Lift each biscuit by hand and roll the top on a mixture of chopped nuts and sugar or only sugar or only nuts. Bake in a moderate oven for about 10-15 minutes till golden. Instead of rolling them in nuts they may be sprinkled with icing sugar before serving if desired. Store in a tight-fitting jar. The cookies may also be iced with a simple glace or chocolate icing.

QUICK SIMPLE COOKIES

1½ cup sugar

3 eggs

3½ cups flour

1 cup butter/margarine/ghee

1 tsp. vanilla

1 tsp. baking powder

Method

Mix and beat the sugar, shortening, eggs and vanilla well. Sift the flour and baking powder together and then add to the egg mixture. Mix all well and then shape into cookies resembling a large coin. In the centre of each cookie press any cake decoration, raisins, or nuts. Place on a greased baking tray and bake in a moderate oven for 7–8 minutes.

BISCUIT OMELET

4 eggs separated

2½ tblsp. castor sugar

Pinch of salt

2 tblsp. flour

Filling:

5 oz. butter

1 egg yolk

7 tsp. cocoa

3½ oz. icing sugar

Method

Whip egg whites with salt till stiff. Cream the yolks with the castor sugar till like custard. Add the flour slowly till well blended. Next add the stiffly beaten egg whites and gently mix. Grease and flour a baking sheet or a Swiss roll tin and spread the mixture not too thin. Bake in a moderately hot oven for about 8-10 mins. When ready take out of oven and gently loosen with a broad knife or spatula by going under the biscuit while still hot. Roll like a Swiss roll. When cold, unroll. Spread filling and roll again. Sprinkle with icing sugar. Alternatively spread with cocoa icing.

Filling:

Put all the ingredients in a saucepan and cook in a double boiler or over a pan of hot water till it thickens slightly and can be easily spread on the biscuit without being runny.

Cocoa Icing:

2 oz. butter

3½ oz. sugar

2 tsp. cocoa

½ cup water

Mix butter and cocoa. Cook sugar with water stirring, if necessary, with only a wooden spoon till resembles thread – when dropped from a spoon it should drip and then break. Add sugar mixture to the cocoa mixture and mix again with a wooden spoon till spreading consistency is reached. Spread this over the rolled and filled biscuit.

LIGHT VANILLA CRESCENT COOKIES

8 oz. flour

4 oz. castor sugar

2 eggs

1 tsp. level (or a little less) baking powder

1 tsp. vanilla essence

7 oz. butter or margarine

4 oz. almonds or hazel nuts chopped fine

Decoration:

1 tblsp. icing sugar

½ tsp. vanilla powder

Method

Sift flour and baking powder together. Add sugar, vanilla, eggs, butter, and almonds. Mix all together. if the dough is sticky put in the refrigerator for a while. Do not use extra flour or the cookies will become heavy. When dough is ready for rolling take out and make several long rolls like bread sticks. They should be the thickness of an average finger. Cut off 5 cm pieces from the rolls. Twist the ends and form into crescent shapes. Bake in a hot oven light brown for about 5-10 minutes. While still hot, roll in a mixture of icing sugar and vanilla powder. Store in a container with a tight-fitting lid. The vanilla crescents will keep for a month stored in this way. If vanilla powder is not available add another ¼ tsp vanilla essence to the cookie mixture.

MARZIPAN POTATOES

500 gm. almonds peeled and ground to a paste

400 gm. powdered castor sugar

5-6 tblsp. unsweetened chocolate powder

Method

Put almond paste and half the sugar in a pan and cook on low heat till the paste leaves the sides of the pan and does not stick to the bottom. Take off heat and cool. Add rest of the sugar and mix well with a wooden spoon or in the food processor for about 1-2 minutes. Grease hands and make into small balls. Spread chocolate powder on a flat dish. Cut three tiny pieces out of the top of the balls with a knife to form a pattern. Now roll balls in the chocolate. Make a few more balls with the cut pieces.

NANKHATAI (I)

(These classic age-old Indian cookies are Muslim in origin and make excellent accompaniments with tea or coffee. They are extremely popular and can be stored for a long period in a container with a tight-fitting lid.)

250 gm. vegetable ghee (*vanaspati*) 250 gm. powdered sugar

750 gm. white flour ¾ tsp. sodium-bicarbonate

Raisins or cashew/peanuts for garnish (optional)

Method

Beat the ghee and sugar till smooth. Sift the flour and soda-bi-carb together and add to the ghee mixture. Gradually mix with hands or the food processor till all well blended. Make into small balls the size of a squash or ping-pong ball. Make a slight depression in the centre with the thumb and press down a raisin or nut well into the nankhatai. No need to make the depression in the centre if not using raisins and nuts. Instead flatten the balls very lightly with the palms. Place the nankhatais on a greased and floured baking tray, brush tops with a little milk to give a shine and bake in a moderate oven for about 10 mins or till done. It should have a mild golden colour. Cool on a wire tray before storing.

Note

Butter can be substituted in place of ghee.

NANKHATAI (II)

250 gm. flour

250 gm. fine semolina

250 gm. ghee

250 gm. chickpea flour (*besan*)

250 gm. sugar powdered

Raisins and nuts as above (optional)

Method

Sift flour, chick-pea flour and semolina. Beat sugar and ghee till smooth. Add to the sifted dry ingredients and blend well gradually, either with hands or in the food processor. Shape and proceed as above. These may also be stored in a container with a tight-fitting lid for a period of time.

KHOURABIA

(This is a Middle Eastern/Israeli version of the Indian Nankhatai. It is equally delicious and can be stored as the above.)

250 gm. any fat (Crisco/margarine/butter etc.	250 gm. castor or fine sugar
500 gm. flour shifted	2 tblsp. anise, powdered cinnamon, cloves, or vanilla etc.

Method

Beat the fat well with the sugar till smooth. – around 5 minutes in an electric blender or processor. Add the flour and the flavouring used. Mix well with hands or in the food processor. Shape like the *nankhatais*. Stick a clove in the centre and place in a greased and floured tray. Bake in a very low oven till done. Can brush the top with milk during the last few minutes of cooking to give it a shine.

GINGER COOKIES

3 eggs separated

3-4 oz. flour sifted

6 oz. castor or, powdered sugar

1-2 tsp. (or more) ginger powder

Method

Beat the yolks of the eggs with the sugar till thick and lemon colored. Beat the egg whites stiff and add to the yolk mixture mixing well. Sift flour and ginger powder together and then fold gradually into the egg mixture stirring continuously to blend evenly. Spread mixture on a greased and floured cookie sheet and bake in a low oven for approx ½ hour or till done. Whilst still hot cut in squares or in diamond shapes. Leave to cool on the sheet. Store in an air-tight jar and keep in a cool place. These cookies remain fresh for a long time.

GINGER THINS -- COOKIES

1½ cup flour sifted

½ tsp. cinnamon powder

½ tsp clove powder

1 cup brown sugar

1 egg beaten

½ tsp. baking soda

½ tsp ginger powder

¼ tsp. salt

12 oz. margarine

¼ cup molasses

Method

Sift the flour with all the dry ingredients once again except sugar. Beat the sugar and margarine. Add to it all the rest of the ingredients and mix till smooth. If dough is too soft add a little more margarine. Grease a baking sheet or tray and drop the dough by ½ coffee spoonfuls on it leaving enough space in between for the cookies to spread. Bake in a medium low oven for 5-6 minutes or till ready.

MARIA'S COOKIES

350 gm. flour

3 egg yolks

350 gm. castor sugar

150 gm. butter/any shortening or, 100 gm. oil

Method

Mix all the above ingredients together. Roll out ¼" thick. Cut into shapes. Bake in a moderate oven. Turn over onto a wire rack to cool. Store in a jar with a tight lid till required.

GLOSSARY

Ajinomoto	Monosodium glutamate (MSG)
Aloo	Potato
Aubergine	Brinjal or egg plant
Ahrar dal	Yellow lentil. Also known as 'tuvar'
Au gratin	A dish quoted with sauce, sprinkled with cheese and crumbs browned in oven or under grill
Barfi, burfi	Dry and sugary Indian confectionary
Bati-charchari	Another type of dry Bengali curry
Beorek	A Middle Eastern pastry dish
Bhapa	Steamed Indian food
Brinjal	Eggplant or aubergine
Bhujia	Dry fried or oven roasted mixed savoury nuts, lentils etc.
Biryani (Biriani)	A special type of 'pilau' usually cooked with meat
Borgul	Cracked wheat
Bori	Shaped and sun-dried balls or lumps of lentils
Casserole	Slow cooked food in a covered heat-proof dish in oven or the utensil itself for such
Chanchra	Bengali dry curry of assorted vegetables
Chapatti	Or roti, handmade, usually round, flat unleavened bread
Charchari	Dry Bengali vegetarian curry
Channa	Cottage cheese similar to 'paneer'

Chenchki	Another type of Bengali dry vegetarian curry
Chop suey	"Mixed spice" in Chinese – an American dish of meat (chicken, beef, pork, prawn) cooked quickly with vegetables
Cholar dal	Lentil made out of split brown peas
Crepe	Word of French origin, fine pancake
Curry powder	A mixture of various Indian spices often used for making curries (commercially available)
Daab	Green coconut
Dal	Any Indian lentil usually with the specific type mentioned before e.g., moong dal
Dalia	Broken wheat used as porridge and in various other dishes
Dalna	Bengali curry with gravy
Dárazsfeszek	Sweet pastry of Hungarian origin
Doi	Yogurt
Dolma	Stuffed vegetable
Dum	Vegetable normally cooked under pressure
Eggplant	Aubergine, brinjal
Escalopes	Flattened meat or fish
Falafel	A Middle Eastern snack
Fettucine	A type of Italian flat pasta
Flambé	A dish, sprinkled with spirit, set alight before serving
Flan	An open tart filled with fruit, cream, custard etc
Galantine	French dish with meat or poultry served cold covered with aspic

Ghonto	A 'mushy' Bengali vegetarian (sometimes non vegetarian) curried dish
Granola	Cereal mixture made of many nutritious items
Gulab jamun	A very popular fried Indian sweet in syrup, brown in colour
Hilsa	Very popular migratory ocean fish caught in the rivers of Bengal delta, akin to 'shad' of the Americas
Hulwa	Also known as Hulva. Soft Indian sweet
Jackfruit	A tropical fruit eaten raw when ripe or cooked while green as a vegetable.
Jhaal	A Bengali curry with chilli hot gravy. Also, peppery or chilli hot
Jhole	Bengali stew
Kalia	A rich and spicy Bengali curry
Kalo Jam	Indian black berry growing in a large tree, supposed to have medicinal properties
Khasta	Indian flaky pastry
Kheer	Indian milk dessert
Kitchri	A mixed rice and lentil preparation
Kochuri	Indian snack of wheat casing and vegetable, lentil (sometimes meat) stuffing usually fried in round shapes
Kofta	Ground meat, fish, or vegetable ball
Korma	A type of rich meat/fish/vegetable curry
Langosh	Or 'Langosch; Hungarian savoury cake
Lo-mien	Chinese dish with noodles, vegetables, meat, shrimps, seafood, and wontons.

Ma	My mother-in-law, Nilima Ghosh, who had a small repertoire of some very tasty dishes.
Malai	Cream of milk
Malpoa	Bengali fried sweet pancake in syrup
Methi	Fenugreek
Meringue	Small pâtisserie made from egg white and sugar
Mishti	Bengali sweets in general
Moong	A green lentil
Moussaka	A meat and egg-plant preparation of Greek origin
Mousse	A cold souffle
Mowcha	Flower of banana plant eaten all over Southeast Asia and Bengal
Mummy	My mother, Ratnavali Baruah, who was a great cook and the daughter of Pragna Sundari Devi the writer of the ground-breaking cook book in Bengali
Pakhi	My sister, Lalitha Jauhar, from whom I learned some Punjabi dishes
Paneer	Another name for 'channa' or cottage cheese
Paratha	Handmade Indian shallow fried bread
Pulao	Also known as Pilau. A rich rice dish
Rasam	South Indian sour soup and eaten as a starter
Riki	My son, Dr. Richik Ghosh; a reasonably good cook, who developed a few dishes as a student, overseas.
Roti	Chapatti or handmade, usually round, flat unleavened bread.
Rosogolla	A Bengali cottage cheese ball in syrup

Saag	Leafy green vegetable e.g. spinach
Sauerkrat	Pickled cabbage of German origin
Sambhar	A South Indian spicy lentil preparation
Sandesh	A dry Bengali confectionary sweet made mainly with cottage cheese
Singara	A pyramid shaped savoury pastry (fried or baked) usually filled with curried items. Also known as 'samosa'.
Sara	My maid, who surprised us with some of her innovations in cooking
Sembe	Swahili word meaning coarse ground maize
Sorsé	Indian mustard or 'rape' seed
Stella mashi	My mother's friend, Stella Das, and a great cook.
Sukiyaki	A dish of Japanese origin
Sushi	Any fresh raw food dish – Japanese origin
Tarkari	A dry Bengali curry
Tengri	Leg or leg bone of animals (usually goats)
Teriyaki	A Japanese cooking technique where food is broiled or grilled in a special sweet soya sauce
Thore	Soft inside of the trunk of a banana plant – a popular vegetable of Bengal (rhymes with 'more')
Tortes	Open tart or rich cake type mixture baked in a pastry case
Zucchini	A vegetable also known as courgette

ALPHABETICAL LIST OF RECIPES

Recipe	Page
Ambrosia	106
Baked Banana Splits	61
Baked Guava Pudding	88
Baked or Pressure-Cooked Stuffed Apples	96
Baked Rosogolla	23
Banana Flambe	60
Basic Ice Cream	111
Bengali Mishti Doi or Sweet Yogurt (I)	82
Besting Cake (German)	167
Bhapa Doi (II)	79
Bhapa Doi (III)	80
Bhapa Doi Or Bengali Steamed Yogurt Dessert (I)	78
Biscuit Omelet	181
Bombé Alaska	107
Bread Hulwa	33
Caramel Meringue with Peaches	52
Carrot Cake	154
Channar Mishti (Bengali Cottage Cheese Sweet)	31
Channar Mishti Roll (Paneer/Cottage-Cheese Sweet Rolls)	30
Chocolate Almond Cake	163
Chocolate Bread Pudding	94
Chocolate Cake	136
Chocolate Cookies	176
Chocolate Ice Cream	114
Chocolate Icebox Cake	158
Chocolate Mousse	67

Recipe	Page
Chocolate Pudding	63
Chocolate Rum Mousse	66
Chocolate Sponge Cake	162
Chocolate Vanilla Cookies	177
Chocolate Wheat Cake	161
Cock-Eyed Eggless Chocolate Cake	165
Coconut Balls	12
Coconut Barfi (I)	9
Coconut Barfi (II)	10
Coconut Barfi (III)	11
Congo Cake	139
Cottage Cheese Dessert	104
Cream Cake (I)	152
Cream Cake (II)	153
Csoroge (Hungarian)	174
Delicious Rice Pudding or Cake	50
Delicious Whole Wheat Spice Cake	160
Dil Bahar	24
Easy Christmas Cake	156
Egg Hulwa	34
Eggless Ice Cream	125
Feather-Weight Sponge	140
Floating Island (Cake)	129
German Apple Cake	135
Ginger Cookies	187
Ginger Marmalade Steam Pudding	85
Ginger Thins -- Cookies	188

Recipe	Page
Guava Kheer	91
Gulab Jamun (I)	25
Gulab Jamun (II)	27
Icebox Christmas Cake	157
Jack Fruit Ice Cream	119
Jalebis	14
Kheer Toast (Cream Toast)	32
Khourabia	186
Lady Kenny	29
Left-Over Frozen Dessert	105
Left-Over Roti Hulwa	40
Lemon Cream	69
Lemon Ice Cream	115
Lemon Pancake Dessert	73
Lemon Sponge Cream	70
Light Vanilla Crescent Cookies	182
Madeleines	150
Malay Dessert	64
Malpoa	44
Mango Ice Cream	117
Mango Kulfi (Indian Eggless Mango Ice Cream)	126
Mango Or Fruit Flan	98
Mango Surprise	97
Marble Cake	132
Maria's Cookies	189
Marzipan Potatoes	183

Recipe	**Page**
Middle Eastern Hulwa (II)	38
Middle Eastern Semolina Hulwa (I)	37
Mishti Doi (II)	83
Mocha Cake	142
Mocha Dessert	77
Mock Ice Cream	124
Mock Shrikhand	84
Nankhatai (I)	184
Nankhatai (II)	185
New Zealand Coconut Ice	13
Nut Cake	137
Okinawa Sweet	45
Orange Cream	102
Orange Cups	101
Orange Flan	99
Orange Or Any Other Fruit Ice Cream	116
Orange Sponge Pudding	87
Oven Sandesh	20
Party Cup Cakes	149
Pastry Almond Cake	166
Patali (Date Jaggery) Cake	164
Patali (Solid Date Jaggery) Ice Cream	122
Pavlova	71
Peach Or Pear Flambé	54
Peanut Ice Cream	121
Pear Dessert	55
Peppermint Ice Cream	120
Pineapple & Ice Cream	59

Recipe	Page
Pineapple Cream Dessert	57
Pineapple Mousse	68
Pineapple Rum Cream Dessert	58
Piquant Melon Dessert	62
Plain Cake with Oil	168
Plain Sponge Cake	147
Plum Dumpling	95
Pound Cake	131
Pressure-Cooked Powder Milk Rosogolla	22
Pudim De Leite (Brazilian Milk Pudding) - Flan	72
Pumpkin Hulwa	35
Quick Easy Sandesh (Iii)	19
Quick Semolina Dessert	51
Quick Simple Cookies	180
Quick-Mix Chocolate Cookies	175
Rangaaloo (Sweet Potato) Pitha (I)	41
Rice Pudding	49
Riki's Bread Pudding	93
Rosogolla	21
Rosomalai Ice Cream	123
Sandesh (II)	18
Sembe (Maize) Cake (Tanzania)	130
Semlor (Swedish Cake)	151
Semolina Barfi	15
Simple Bread Pudding	92
Simple Home-Baked Cookies	179
Simple Ice Cream	112
Simple Sandesh (I)	17

Recipe	Page
Somloi Galuska (A Rich Cake Dessert)	75
Southeast Asian Casava Coconut Cake	169
Soya Barfi	16
Soya Bean Hulwa	36
Soya Powder Gulab Jamun	28
Spiced Wheat Cake	159
Sponge for Tortes	145
Sponge Gateau	141
Steamed Guava or Fruit Pudding	89
Steamed Orange Pudding	86
Stewed Pears	56
Stir Cake	138
Strawberry Delight	133
Strawberry Ice Cream	118
Sweet Potato Hulwa	39
Sweet Potato Mishti (II)	43
Tangy Sponge Cake	144
Tasty Cookies	173
Tri-Coloured Dessert	65
Uncooked Chocolate Biscuits	178
Vanilla Ice Cream	113
Vienna Rolls	143
Winter Sponge Cake	155
Yogurt Toffee or Burfi of Bhapa (Iv)	81

www.ingramcontent.com/pod-product-compliance
Lightning Source LLC
LaVergne TN
LVHW061611070526
838199LV00078B/7242